THE BUILDERS

THE BUILDERS

Six Master Carpenters Who Shaped Louisiana's Antebellum Lafourche Country

DAVID D. PLATER

2026
University of Louisiana at Lafayette Press

ISBN 13 (paper): 978-1-959569-36-7

http://ulpress.org
University of Louisiana at Lafayette Press
P.O. Box 43558
Lafayette, LA 70504-3558

Library of Congress Cataloging-in-Publication Data

Names: Plater, David D. (David Dunboyne), 1936- author
Title: The builders : six master carpenters who shaped Louisiana's antebellum Lafourche country / David D. Plater.
Description: Lafayette, LA : University of Louisiana at Lafayette Press, 2026. | Includes bibliographical references and index.
Identifiers: LCCN 2026008545 | ISBN 9781959569367 paperback
Subjects: LCSH: Carpenters--Louisiana--Lafourche Parish | Buildings--Louisiana--Lafourche Parish--History--19th century | Lafourche Parish (La.)--History--19th century | Lafourche, Bayou (La.)--History--19th century | LCGFT: Biographies
Classification: LCC F377.L25 P53 2026
LC record available at https://lccn.loc.gov/2026008545

cover image: "Thibodeauville Bayou Lafourche," Alfred E. Waud etching of downtown Thibodaux, 1871. Courtesy of the Historic New Orleans Collection, accession 1966.21

This book honors the memory of our family friend George Core, former editor of *The Sewanee Review of Literature*.

Table of Contents

Acknowledgments

The four major sources of information from which this work derives are the Archives and Special Collections division of the Ellender Library at Nicholls State University, protected and managed by archivist Clifton Theriot; the records of the clerk of court of Lafourche Parish, under the direction of Annette Fontana; the office of the clerk of the Thibodaux City Council, administered by Jenny Morvant, who made available to me the early minutes of the city council; and the office of the clerk of the Lafourche Parish Council, managed by Carleen Babin, and where the original minutes and ordinances of the parish council are stored. To all, I offer my appreciation for their invaluable service.

Those who read this work in various stages include my wife, Sheela Burke Plater, whose encouragement and patience are granite on which I stand. I also received comments from and the support of Professor Richard Campanella of the Tulane University School of Architecture. I am indebted to him for taking time from his busy life of teaching and writing to read an early draft of the book and offer good suggestions. The aforementioned archivist at Nicholls State guided me numerous times during research, read the book in its various drafts, and pointed out mistakes that needed my attention. He also assisted with choosing, titling, and scanning illustrations. Clifton Theriot continues to demonstrate the importance of the work of preserving the written and photographic history of the Lafourche country. His associate at the library, IT Specialist William Charron, was invaluable solving some technical issues when putting together drafts. Jackie Jackson provided seemingly vast patience with me and a high level of expertise in reading and editing the manuscript. Finally, my editor at UL Press, Devon Lord, could not have been more involved and organized at all stages of the editing process. I am indebted to her for her patience, persistence, and skill, as well as UL Press production manager, Mary Karnath Duhé, for her work on layout and design of the final drafts of the book.

Others have been more than helpful. DeeDee DiBenedetto directed me to sources which were useful and difficult to find. Jo Norton, a descendant of the master builder Absalom Kees, gave information about him and cheered me on in the overall task. Laura Browning provided invaluable assistance with the connections between Absalom Kees and William John Minor and with details of the time the master carpenter Edward Truman Burnham spent serving in the United States Army in the Civil War. Civil engineers Leonard Chauvin Jr. and Nicholas Billiot assisted with maps of early Thibodaux, including identifying the course of Bayou Terrebonne from its diversion from Bayou Lafourche. Mary Lou Eichhorn of the Historic New Orleans Collection and Karen Leathham and Erin Patterson of the Louisiana State Museum provided much help in arranging permission to use illustrations. James Sefcik, former director of the Louisiana State Museum, gave me encouragement over the past few years as well. And among the final acts before publication is the creation of the index, a task performed admirably by Cynthia Landeen.

List of Images

Preface

The physical setting of this work is primarily the Lafourche region, also called the Lafourche country of Louisiana, and particularly the Lafourche parish seat, Thibodaux, incorporated in 1838. The area is dominated by Bayou Lafourche, an ancient main trunk, then distributary, of the Mississippi River. Eons ago, the Mississippi River changed course, taking a more easterly route and creating the distributary called Bayou Lafourche. The Lafourche remnant stream split off from the Mississippi River at today's river town of Donaldsonville. Smaller streams, like Bayou Terrebonne, diverged from Bayou Lafourche. The region thus has its own large delta system and special topography of streams, swamps, and fertile farmland. Because of a dam built at the mouth of the bayou in the early 1900s, seasonal Mississippi River floods no longer plague the populations of the Lafourche country.

The book is about six master carpenters or builders who came to Louisiana from other states during the nation's antebellum period and lived and practiced their crafts in the Lafourche region. They shaped the look and character of Lafourche, Terrebonne, and Assumption Parish towns and countryside, especially in and around the bayou-side settlement of Thibodaux, a thriving regional hub before the American Civil War.

To my knowledge, no such historical work has been written about similar south Louisiana bayou communities. Of comparable settlements in antebellum southeast Louisiana, best exemplified by New Iberia, Franklin, and Houma, some studies exist. Prominent for Franklin are the 1972 publication by Florence Blackburn and Fay G. Brown, *Franklin through the Years,* and the excellent genealogy of early Franklin families, *A Family Montage,* published in 2002 and written by Thomas Frere Kramer. For New Iberia, there is the assemblage of vignettes by Glenn R. Conrad, *New Iberia: Essays on the Town and Its People* (1979, second edition 1986). And for Houma, an important work was authored by Christopher E. Cenac Sr. and Claire Domangue Joller, *Hard Scrabble to Hallelujah: Legacies of Terrebonne Parish,*

Louisiana (Volume 1: Bayou Terrebonne), published in 2016. Although not per se about Houma, *Hard Scrabble to Hallelujah* has provided resources for study of the early plantations on each side of Bayou Terrebonne, which runs through the town. None of these works included much information about the men who, in the literal sense, constructed those areas' diverse private and public buildings before the Civil War.[1]

Little has been published and made widely available about the first half of Thibodaux's nineteenth-century past. After the Civil War, *The Weekly Thibodaux Sentinel* newspaper's longtime publisher and frequent local politician, Silas Grisamore, wrote articles in the 1890s about the antebellum town; they are available on microfilm and more recently a transcription of his articles under the name S. T. Grisamore, titled "Lafourche Parish Louisiana, Thibodaux of 1840s," was published online through Genealogy Trails and History Group, transcribed and submitted by a volunteer named Savanna. Some of the articles also are reprinted in William Littlejohn Martin's *Records and Recollections of Thibodaux, Louisiana* (Philip D. Uzée, comp.), using the William Littlejohn Martin Collection of the Nicholls State University Archives. *"The Remarkably Neat Church in the Village of Thibodaux": An Antebellum History of St. John's Episcopal Church* (1994, reprint 2016) was edited and partially written by this author and contributed to by others. It is about one antebellum Protestant Episcopal church, St. John's, designed by Bishop Leonidas Polk and constructed from 1843 to 1844 by two Thibodaux builders, Absalom Kees and James Frost. Their stories, as well as those of the church founders, are outlined in the book, which also attempts to provide the historical setting for the church's establishment. It does not pursue St. John's builders' other contributions to the town and region. The identities of the 1856 St. John's renovation architect and builder, Henry Howard and E. T. Burnham, respectively, were not yet known when "*The Remarkably Neat Church in the Village of Thibodaux*" first appeared. In 1987, Philip D. Uzee used a number of his columns in the Thibodaux *Daily Comet* to write a short work, *Thibodaux Chronicles: A Sesquicentennial History.* That book concentrates mainly on the town's life from the beginning of the Civil War to the time of its publication.[2]

The four south Louisiana towns of Thibodaux, Houma, Franklin, and New Iberia all were settlements on navigable bayous located in different parts of the historical deltas of the Mississippi River. They all became early governmental seats of their parishes. All thrived through most of the nineteenth century, particularly as centers of sugarcane agriculture and sugar manufacture. All featured mixes of inhabitants from various historical and cultural backgrounds. And all took inspiration for much of their antebellum architecture from the classical Greek and Roman building styles that gained such popularity in the upper Mississippi and Ohio Valleys and northeast and southern parts of the United States and to which was added Gothic Revival after 1850.[3]

Many structures from the antebellum years, dating from Louisiana's 1812 statehood to 1861, survive in and near those communities. The published town histories of Franklin and New Iberia do not include the men who built the homes, mills, and other business establishments that so distinguished those communities. Most references to "builders" are to those who owned the structures, and, as such, commissioned the actual contractors. We learn little about their architects, if any, or about the artisans, contractors, and other workers, enslaved and free, who fashioned and pieced together the structural timbers, doors, frames, and moldings, laid the brick foundations and walls, and roofed and guttered structures. Just who were these people, where were they from, how had they gained their crafts, where and how did they operate, and where and how did they live? Addressing these questions for Thibodaux and its Lafourche country environs is the focus of this work.

Much information about the craftsmen of our early bayou communities is lost or was never documented. For Thibodaux and environs, this effort has relied upon public records in the Thibodaux archives in city hall, specifically the early minutes of the town council dating from 1838. In addition, antebellum Lafourche Parish police jury minutes and statutes and the clerk of court records from Assumption Parish, Lafourche Parish, and Terrebonne Parish have filled needs. Lafourche has been useful for information in civil suits and in recorded building contracts held in its administrative office as well as in that of the parish clerk of court. Local newspapers were published from an early date, some issues of which have been microfilmed. *The Thibodaux Minerva* newspaper, available mainly from 1853 to 1856, is of help, as are Silas T. Grisamore's aforementioned articles in *The Weekly Thibodaux Sentinel*.[4] The lack of personal documents of the master carpenters and other craftsmen, such as letters, diaries, and ledgers, has been a drawback. If the artisans kept records of their lives and businesses, little so far has been located outside of public records.

Will we now approach a better understanding of the richness of regional life in an old and important part of Louisiana? That is the hope.

The author's wish, too, is to stimulate other studies about the people of the early Lafourche, Terrebonne, and Teche regions, whose marks on their Louisiana communities and countryside were long-lasting but whose stories await scrutiny.

CHAPTER ONE

Early Years in the Lafourche Country

The early maps of the Mississippi River and her distributaries in southeast Louisiana reveal how much time and prodigious human and ox-animal labor took place in the initial stages of European settlement. The maps show mainly narrow spaces of inhabited and cultivated land between edges of streams and the dense forests. The process of clearing required many years and great effort, and farms remained small well into the nineteenth century. Developing crops and outgrowing villages into towns progressed at a torturously slow pace.[1]

Bayou Lafourche's geological origins as the primary trunk and then as a main distributary of the Mississippi River stretch back several thousand years. Wind and water eroded rock and soil each year; sand, silt, and clay carried by rivers from an enormous section of North America were deposited gradually across broad and varying swaths of the current southern parts of Louisiana. As the soil and rock particles created land, heavier sand dropped out of solution closest to a river's main stream. Predominantly abundant silt came out of solution farther away from the river, and light clay particles were deposited farthest away. As a result, the closer-to-main-stream soil deposits from floods formed what are colloquially known as ridges, with land elevations higher than where each of the other soils was laid down. The clay soil areas of lowest elevation, called backswamps, were the most distant from the rivers and distributary bayous. "Old Man River" shifted course occasionally, forming separate, distinct deltas; each time, the older bayou banks away from active flood zones became populated by Indigenous peoples.[2]

In the last half of the eighteenth century, families of European strains began to arrive. French-speaking Acadians, expelled by Great Britain from Nova Scotia, landed in Louisiana primarily via France and England, some Caribbean islands, and places along the Atlantic Coast of Britain's American colonies. They came in waves beginning in the 1760s; then, during the 1780s and the Spanish occupation of the Lafourche region, people who had resided

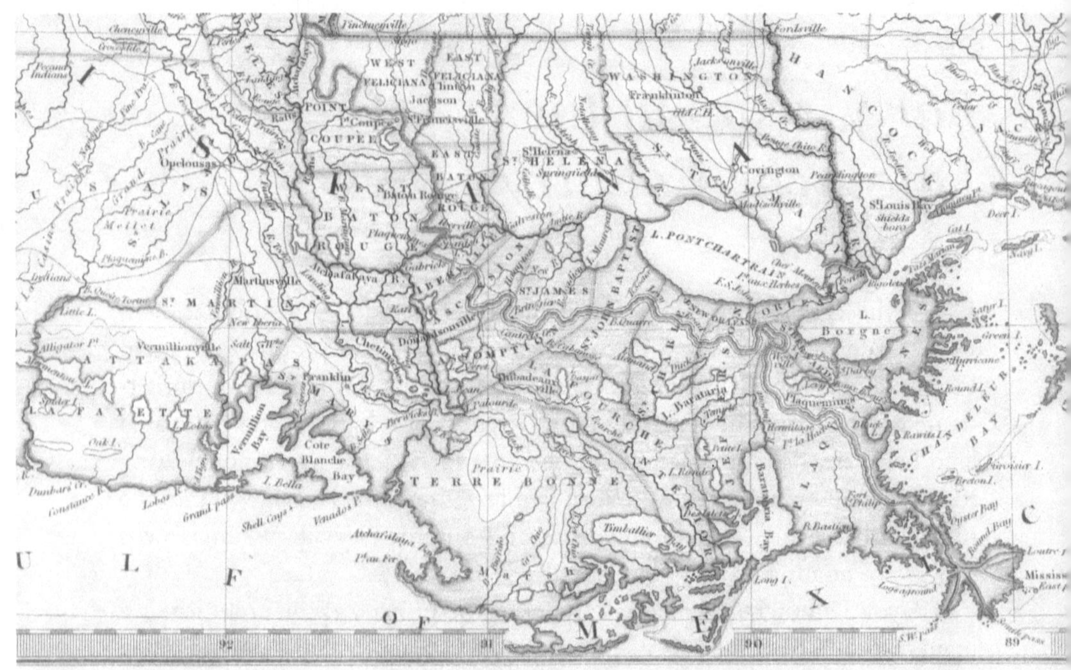

IMAGE 1. Early map of southeast Louisiana showing the Lafourche, Terrebonne, and Teche regions of the old Mississippi River Delta. Courtesy Nicholls State University Archives.

for years in France following their expulsion from Nova Scotia migrated in seven ships to Louisiana. Upon landing alongside the Mississippi River, the settlers made their way down Bayou Lafourche from the old town of Donaldsonville in what is now Ascension Parish. Added to by newly-arriving refugees from European wars in the late eighteenth and early nineteenth centuries, as well as others, the colonists became established along both sides of Bayous Lafourche and Terrebonne and to the areas below today's Lockport and Houma. Few enslaved Africans could be counted among the mostly small farmers living alongside the two bayous. These immigrants traded primarily in locally-grown crops like corn and cotton. Undertaken using small watercraft navigating between the Lafourche countryside and New Orleans, their commerce thrived in the years before 1800. The varied watercraft negotiated mainly interior bayou and lake passages to the Mississippi River's west bank to reach the growing city.

The Acadians' habitations and barns at first resembled the structures of their European and Canadian rural origins, heavily built of post-and-beam and half-timber, but gradually changed as experience in a new climate and place required. Porches to protect the house fronts and L- and T-wings off the house rears developed. For roofs, cypress shingles from the locale instead of heavy, unsuitable grass and dirt were used. Weather-protected interior chimneys, rather than those attached onto the outsides of exterior walls, tended to be built in the bayou country.[3]

Spain, which owned the Lafourche area in the latter part of the eighteenth century, provided land grants to immigrants; peopling the bayou banks with farmers was considered a protective barrier to help prevent British encroachment on Spain's older possessions to the west. Americans from the Eastern Seaboard and upper South added to the mix of settlers along Bayous Lafourche and Terrebonne, their flow increasing after 1800 and particularly after the War of 1812. The Americans, sometimes called "Anglos," arrived by dugouts, canoes, flatboats, and small luggers called *caboteurs*. Then, as the Assumption Parish planter William W. Pugh described, in the spring of 1825 "great was the wonder of the inhabitants" when "the old steamer Eagle made her appearance on the Lafourche under the command of Captain [Ferdinand M.] Streck" of Donaldsonville.[4] The new steam energy technology would transform the bayou country. Aided by ready credit from a growing number of regional branch banks, such as the New Orleans-based Union Bank of Louisiana, the rapidly-increasing Anglo-American population bought up the fertile land and undertook a commercial form of agriculture. The newer farms at first grew and ginned cotton, followed soon by sugarcane agriculture and the manufacture of raw sugar. As was the case along the Mississippi River, land parcels enlarged, and many planters of Acadian descent took up the new farming model. Especially after 1820, the planters introduced enslaved workers, most of them brought from other states in the American South; thus, the slave trade was introduced to "the Lafourche Interior," as the old delta region of Bayous Lafourche and Terrebonne was at first named. Despite the use of improved levees to hold back the seasonal high water, flooding plagued settlers along Bayou Lafourche and elsewhere in the Mississippi Valley during the 1800s.

Bayou Teche, an even earlier, well-established center for Acadians, people of Spanish origin, and then for Americans, deserves to be mentioned in comparison to Bayou Lafourche. Not directly tied to the Mississippi River,

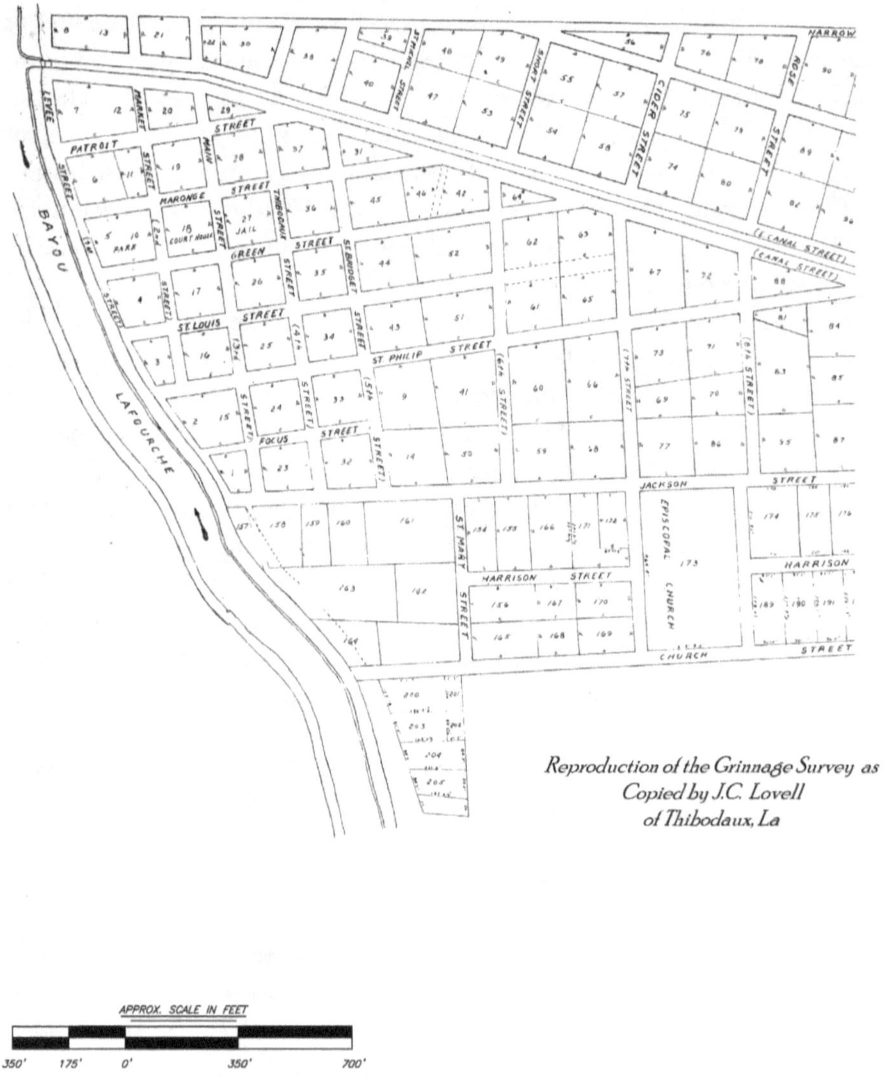

Reproduction of the Grinnage Survey as Copied by J.C. Lovell of Thibodaux, La

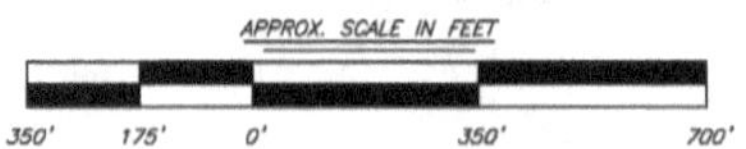

IMAGE 2. Survey map of the early village of Thibodaux (James B. Grinage, surveyor), 1842; copy by J. C. Lovell. Courtesy of Leonard Chauvin Jr. and Nicholas Billiot.

but also an earlier course of the vast, continent-long Mississippi, Bayou Teche served mainly small passenger vessels like rowboats early on, expanding soon to sailing vessels. After 1825, steamboats also ministered to both Franklin and New Iberia as part of a trade in cotton and sugar destined for

New Orleans. One common passage, accessible during floodtime and traveled to and from the Mississippi River at the town of Plaquemine, employed the distributary, known as Bayou Plaquemine, and the lakes and smaller bayous found throughout the Atchafalaya Basin to reach Bayou Teche. Another increasingly utilized route for carrying people and goods was itself the Atchafalaya River, joined by Bayou Teche at Brashear's Landing (now named Morgan City). Sailing or steam vessels found that they could proceed via the Atchafalaya to the Gulf of Mexico, then head east to the mouth of the Mississippi River and thus to New Orleans.[5]

In 1812, Louisiana designated a tiny group of habitations as the seat of government of Lafourche Parish: a future village, officially to be called Thibodaux. Then only a sparsely-populated agricultural settlement on the right-descending or west bank of Bayou Lafourche, about forty miles from its head at Donaldsonville, at first it barely grew. In 1820, two men of European descent owned the land on which the village was to be founded. Just upstream from the soon-to-be town center, Francois Himmel (or Himel), a Louisiana native, farmed a three-arpent-wide[6] tract fronting on the bayou. His property's lower, or downstream, edge was where today's Jackson Street, named for the hero of the Battle of New Orleans in 1815, is located.

Prior to its renaming, Jackson Street was referred to as the Terrebonne Road. Like all nineteenth-century roads along Bayou Lafourche, the Terrebonne Road—at first a raw, overgrown path—remained little more than a dirt wagon road. It connected Bayou Lafourche with the navigable upper end of Bayou Terrebonne, approximately at the intersection of today's Jackson Street with Canal Boulevard. Long before Europeans arrived in Louisiana, Bayou Terrebonne had silted in where it branched off Bayou Lafourche, at the beginning of today's Ridgefield Road at St. Mary Street (now LA Highway 1). The bayou snaked south through what became the Ridgefield Annex section of town around 1905. A vestige of the original channel is visible on an aerial photograph created by the US Department of Agriculture in 1940.

The village's namesake, Henry Schuyler Thibodaux, acquired a farm fronting on Bayou Lafourche below Himmel's farm and the Terrebonne Road in January 1818. The tract stretched from the Terrebonne Road five blocks down to Maronge Street, on the eastern edge of the town's courthouse square. The recorded sale described Thibodaux's acquisition as "about six arpents [more exactly, 5¾ arpents, or 1,104 feet] in the front with the depth of forty arpents [7,680 feet] and fronting on the bayou Lafourche, at the bayou Darbonne [Terrebonne]." The consideration, $3,000, was "payable at different times" to Henry Johnson, a native of Virginia who moved to the Territory of Orleans in 1809. At the time of the naming of Franklin as the seat of government for St. Mary Parish, Johnson became St. Mary's first judge. Soon a prominent politician and land speculator, Johnson had acquired the Lafourche property from one Joseph Malbrough in 1813. The portion of Johnson's farm closest to Bayou Lafourche developed into the central business district of the new village of Thibodaux.

Another parcel of land, owned by one Hugh Johnston, lay just downstream from the farm (and future commercial tract) that Henry S. Thibodaux bought from Henry Johnson. Fronting two to three arpents "on Lafourche," it was sold to Henry S. Thibodaux on March 20, 1813. The compensation was "a certain negro woman, called Phyllis, and her

IMAGE 3. US Department of Agriculture aerial photo CPV-3A-62, tracing source of Bayou Terrebonne from Bayou Lafourche to its intersection with current Canal Blvd., Thibodaux, December 9, 1940. Courtesy of Leonard Chauvin Jr. and Nicholas Billiot.

child, called Bob, which I [Johnston] have agreed to take in payment for the said land."[7] The property's downstream edge was approximately where today's Narrow Street is located.

As of 1820, therefore, Henry Schuyler Thibodaux was, or remained, owner of all land between Francois Himmel's tract and Jackson Street on down to Narrow Street, fronting on Bayou Lafourche and extending to the rear about forty arpents. Prior owners had cleared a thin land strip already alongside the bayou, and this parcel backed up to poorly drained forests of mixed hardwood and cypress trees. What was to be the use of the land obtained by Henry S. Thibodaux? There was no question that he wanted to create a town on his property. He found just the right person to help him with the layout: a young surveyor and native of Virginia named James Boyd Grinage.[8]

CHAPTER TWO

Life Along the Bayou
The Village

A son of Aaron Grinage and Ruth Strout, who married in 1790 in North Carolina, James B. Grinage was born in 1801 in Georgia. The family eventually ended up in St. Helena Parish, Louisiana, northeast of Baton Rouge.[1] A land surveyor before the age of twenty, Grinage gained employment in 1820 from Henry S. Thibodaux to create the first plat of the brand-new village. No copy of the plat remains. Grinage had been made a deputy surveyor in the US Public Land Survey System and eventually became the parish surveyor for Lafourche. He liked the village of Thibodaux, and in 1828 Grinage invested in a lot, 70 feet by 140 feet, which he acquired from Ingoe Dozer.[2] The purchase was probably in celebration of matrimony: that year, Grinage married Louisiana Kar of Thibodaux.[3]

What sort of place did James Boyd Grinage and other immigrants to the new community of Thibodaux find? It remained tiny well past the 1825 date assigned by planter William W. Pugh as the first use of Bayou Lafourche for steamboat service; the village numbered only about one hundred people in 1830. It had already begun to change, however, from a largely French-speaking Acadian settlement to one of mixed cultures and languages. In illustration, in 1829 several Anglo-American entrepreneurs, mainly Dr. James A. Scudday, John C. Beatty, Joseph Chandler, and Richard G. Ellis, formed an enterprise named the Lafourche and Terrebonne Navigation Company. In 1830, it acquired a strip of land one hundred feet wide near the lower side of the village, connecting Bayou Lafourche to the still-navigable upper Bayou Terrebonne, together with four village lots at the Bayou Lafourche-end of the strip. The property donation from Brigitte Belanger Thibodaux, who had been widowed by Henry S. Thibodaux's death on October 4, 1827, stated that the purpose was "to encourage the company . . . and in the same order to enhance her own interests in the town of Thibodauxville."[4] Noted as being part of the community property with her deceased husband, the land was valued at $4,000. Both Madame Thibodaux and the canal company president,

Richard Ellis, owned sugar plantations only a few miles down Bayou Terrebonne from the new canal.

Assigned by the state of Louisiana a width of twenty-five feet, the Lafourche and Terrebonne Navigation Company soon ordered a modest-sized canal dug.[5] Its leaders quickly realized that trade through the canal needed a warehouse for storing goods readied for transfer between canal boats and steam-operated vessels on Bayou Lafourche. They achieved this necessity in 1831, when the company sold to John Sargent and Alexander Lawson a corner plot fronting on Bayou Lafourche and Henry Clay Street (on the upper or west side of the canal). The contract obligated the buyers to construct a "commodious warehouse for storage" within six months. Hitherto joined to Bayou Terrebonne only by wagon road, Bayou Lafourche and her new settlement became united by water directly to Bayou Terrebonne. The canal and warehouse construction immediately encouraged trade growth to and from the agriculturally rich country to the southwest of Thibodaux.[6]

After two unsuccessful attempts in 1830 and 1832, the village leaders achieved incorporation by an act of the Louisiana legislature, approved by Governor E. D. White in March 1838. Brigitte Belanger Thibodaux owned

IMAGE 4. The Lafourche and Terrebonne Navigation Canal, Postbellum View. Courtesy of Nicholls State University Archives.

many of the numbered town lots shown on the Grinage plat and actively promoted the community's growth (and her wealth) through lot sales and donations. According to the postbellum editor of *The Weekly Thibodaux Sentinel*, Silas Grisamore, at the end of the 1830s the village had achieved a respectable population of around five hundred, but the settlement remained challenged.[7]

The first, unanimously elected mayor after incorporation was the Kentucky native James McAllister, a respected, popular district judge. Of the town's eligible population, forty-six cast votes to elect four "trustees," as council members were known: they were Mathurin Bourg, Dr. James A. Scudday, John C. Beatty, and Alexander Lawson. Serious, long-existing matters required the early, successive town mayors' and councils' attentions. The antebellum minutes of Thibodaux council meetings tell a story of concerns and slow progress, not just for those first years but throughout the era.[8]

Except for some urban expansion south along the new canal and on Jackson Street, as of the late 1830s, most Thibodaux business, government, and inhabited structures were intermixed and situated within the first few streets from the bank of Bayou Lafourche. The village design had a formality due to the crisscross of streets, and even as the town spread south, east, and west (northward development was blocked by Bayou Lafourche), the downtown retained that quality. Buildings until the mid-1840s were predominantly one or one-and-a-half story and sturdily wooden-frame built, the walls filled between thick studs with a mix of mud and moss, chimneys likewise of mud and moss; and residences kept a traditional Creole/Acadian style. Brick slowly began replacing mud and moss in center or interior side chimneys and also replaced cypress wood post (sections of tree trunks) piers. Most habitations possessed broad galleries in front, side-facing gables, two entrance doors, and steeply slanted cypress shake roofs. Cooking took place outdoor under shed roofs, or kitchens and additional living rooms might be attached in L-shape or T-shape to the main house. Alternatively, modest wood-frame kitchens were located in separate walled structures, containing wood-fueled iron stoves. Simple, "one- or two-holer" privies, often called *necessaries*, were erected over shallow pits dug in the rear or side yards of dwellings. Although inhabitants traditionally washed clothes in Bayou Lafourche, they increasingly collected water for drinking and washing or bathing from rainwater that flowed into V-shaped cypress-plank gutters along the bottom edges of cypress shake roofs. The runoff then was directed into wooden barrels or cisterns. As noted by the planter William W. Pugh

IMAGE 5. Acadian-style nineteenth-century homes in Thibodaux. Courtesy of Nicholls State University Archives.

of Assumption Parish, glass windows were rare alongside Bayou Lafourche; window openings only received protection against the elements and insects from heavy wooden shutters. Screening awaited the early twentieth century.[9]

If humble, the early village combined winning features: an adjacent navigable bayou connecting it to the Mississippi River and so to New Orleans; from 1808, her status as the Lafourche Parish seat of government; a platted town lot layout that allowed for managed growth; and the newly dug, privately-financed navigation canal between Bayou Lafourche and Bayou Terrebonne. Thibodaux seemed destined to become a major regional center of commerce.

The town politicians struggled with numerous issues relating to the growth of Thibodaux. To begin, it needed to accommodate watercraft moorings alongside the busy bayou frontage; the arrangements had been haphazard, unregulated, and uncontrolled. For years, numerous flatboats sought places to tie up, and an increasing number of steamboats had been venturing down the bayou from the Mississippi River to pick up and drop off travelers and goods. Almost immediately after incorporation in 1838, the council set aside space for docking, loading, and unloading steamboats on the bayou bank from St. Philip Street to the area downstream in front of the courthouse square, just above Maronge Street. Although at first the city government disallowed various commercial craft like small schooners and other sailboats, as well as flatboats, soon the council established rules for handling flatboats and other watercraft "laying at the levee" within the town limits. A wharf master was appointed to regulate moorings and to exact fines for violation of rules.[10]

Some comparison between this Bayou Lafourche scene and that along her sister stream, Bayou Teche, and the so-called Attakapas country west of Thibodaux again may be helpful. Similar to Bayou Lafourche historically in having once been a major course of the Mississippi River, small passenger vessels like rowboats and pirogues navigated Bayou Teche, then expanded to sailing vessels. After steamboats arrived, mainly hauling cotton and sugar destined for New Orleans, the watercraft served both Franklin, the seat of St. Mary Parish, and upstream New Iberia, the seat of Iberia Parish.

An early shipping route to and from the Teche, which was especially accessible during flood time, branched off the Mississippi River at the town of Plaquemine. Called Bayou Plaquemine, the distributary flowed west into and across smaller bayous and lakes in the Atchafalaya Basin to Bayou Teche. Another increasingly utilized passage for vessels carrying goods and people began from Bayou Teche at its junction with the Atchafalaya River and on south to the Gulf of Mexico. The route allowed sailboats and steamboats to continue east to the mouth of the Mississippi River and up to New Orleans. Beginning near Napoleonville, a third route connected Bayou Lafourche to the Atchafalaya River and Bayou Teche. Known as the Attakapas Canal, it ran from the bayou at Napoleonville west to Lake Verret, and from there through various other lakes to the Atchafalaya. The canal was a "main highway" for smaller boats traveling between the Lafourche and Teche regions.[11] Thus, the communities along all three streams made use of trade routes to and from New Orleans to accommodate the steadily improving technology of steam energy. By 1860, rail service connected New Orleans with Bayou Lafourche and, farther to the west, with the Atchafalaya River at Brashear's Landing (today's Morgan City).

In addition to the management of shipping, other improvements in Thibodaux addressed myriad issues that symbolized the prospects for and actual growth of the town. More streets were added when, for instance, in 1842 the trustees continued St. Philip and Green Streets from Bayou Lafourche southward "til they strike the [Lafourche and Terrebonne] Canal." They resolved to extend Cider Street (now West Seventh Street) from Jackson Street to the canal; other streets parallel to and "back from" Cider were to be "left open" to extend from Jackson to the canal. Similar decisions determined routes for most of the streets situated below (east of) the canal. In addition, Brigitte Belanger Thibodaux arranged in 1842 to exchange the old city burial ground in the middle of the business district (its precise site is undocumented) for one on the lower side of and near to the end of the canal. The new one was to be located at lot 149 on the new Grinage survey. Madame Thibodaux was required to fence the new cemetery and "have the bodies of persons buried on the other lot properly removed and buried" on lot 149.[12]

Fire constituted a major problem in a town where most houses were made of wood. Although an organized system of fighting blazes may have existed already, the official, if primitive, beginnings of town-sponsored fire protection came in 1843. The council bought 250 feet of fire hose "of Mr Hoey at eight-one and a quarter cents per foot," and the mayor was authorized "to buy one dozen leather fire buckets not to cost more than three dollars each." That year, too, the master carpenter Absalom Kees completed a fire engine house adjacent to the market house that fronted on Bayou Lafourche, a water well for fire-fighting, and "a trough to wash the engine hose in, the pins to suspend the hose, and a pole upon which to hoist and dry the same." Illustrative of the difficulty of fire protection in pre-Civil War Thibodaux, toward the close of the era, the council forbade "the further construction of any new Wooden or Frame Building in the center and business part of the town."[13]

Providing a constant source of public grumbling, most town streets remained unpaved and usually rutted for years after incorporation. Efforts commenced in the early 1840s to cover street sidewalks with bricks or "cockle shells." In one instance, for example, lot owners along the east side of Jackson Street received orders to grade their front sidewalks with sand from the bayou and pave with bricks or shells those in front of their respective lots "not less than four inches thick over the sand." A council committee also received authority to contract for curbing on Jackson Street and "to extend the curbing to the levee."[14]

All such improvements, however, relied upon adequate drainage. The issue plagued the council from the start. Local topography dictated that runoff from rain flowed from the Bayou Lafourche natural ridge away to what the council termed the "low ground in the rear of said town."[15] That rear section, essentially a wooded, swampy area, extended south away from the bayou approximately from Thibodaux Street (now West Fourth Street). The proximity of forest to village showed how constricted the inhabited parts were in relation to low areas. As the Bayou Lafourche planter William W. Pugh observed in a memoir written after the Civil War but referring particularly to an earlier time, "a good forest was looked on as an indispensable adjunct to a plantation."[16] The swampy, wooded areas provided firewood and construction material for habitations and sugarcane mills. In town, the forests thinned out gradually to the south as the settlement developed in the surveyed space between Jackson Street and the canal of the Lafourche and Terrebonne Navigation Canal Company.

In order to manage rain runoff properly, the town required that property owners create streetside ditches in the fronts of their structures. Eventually the council used the new canal leading to Bayou Terrebonne as a destination for the runoff from the main part of town. The trustees directed that all ditches be dug five feet wide at the top, three at the bottom, and to a depth not less than three feet; the ditches must unite in such a way as to "give a free course to the water from the levee to the low ground." Lot owners fronting on streets gained permission to throw the excavated dirt onto their street or sidewalk, but the clods must be "well broken up and levelled." Addressing the need for pedestrian and vehicle crossing of such drains, the council endeavored to construct public bridges in the fronts of homes and businesses; an owner of a corner lot presumably was required by the town government to erect two bridges at the street corner. Enforcing these and similar requirements became an ongoing challenge, almost impossible to meet.[17]

Maintaining the community's health and cleanliness likewise occupied the council. As was common everywhere in mid-nineteenth-century American towns, animals in early Thibodaux were mostly on the loose. Kept for food as well as for pets and work, their sharp calls and smells pervaded the air. People added to the filth from domestic animal excrement by throwing carcasses and other refuse onto streets and sidewalks and into ditches, the bayou, and the new canal.

Such unsanitary routines typified the town when incorporated in 1838 and forced the council to act. The trustees made citizens pen their hogs, a principal source of food, and authorized the town constable to kill any that were found running loose. They also imposed a per-owner limit of two dogs. Neither did they spare goats running in the streets, but these proved especially hard to corral and keep confined. Roaming chickens were and remained omnipresent.

The obstructive and foul animal disposal practices proved intolerable and forced the trustees to find a place for their fellow citizens to dispose of such trash. By 1846, the spot designated as the dumping zone was "that part of Crazy Street [now East Tenth Street], east of President Street . . . for the reception of all dead beasts and other offensive matters." Indicative of the forested nature of the chosen place, the mayor was authorized to "have the timber cleared off of said Streets so as to make it easily accessible." Prompted by the regional presence and ravages of Asiatic cholera in the late 1840s, Thibodaux addressed sanitation issues even on private lots, of which "especially the back lots are in a very filthy condition." The trustees requested every citizen to clean up his lot and his "outer yard." The filth problem was aggravated by the practice of dumping chamber pots in the rear portions of house lots. Town officials provided lime dust, commonly thought to prevent infection, to sprinkle around privies as well as to sprinkle on streets and for whitewashing house fronts during yellow fever plagues. The village's outhouses occasioned such criticism that the city council prohibited their placement any closer than ten feet to sidewalks. In 1856, the city government commenced paying someone to bury dead animals; usually the responsible person was the constable at the time, one George Boner (or Bonner).[18]

Little mention of smoke pollution in early Thibodaux has been found, but house and kitchen fires, smoke from foundries near the downtown, and trash burns all must have contributed to a frequently smoky atmosphere. Fuel sources for homes, businesses, and government buildings began to shift from wood to coal in the 1840s. To those pollutants, one might add smoke from fuel burned in the numerous local sugar mills during cane harvest and grinding, as well as the practice of burning cane to remove leaves. Smoke from trash collection burn sites within and near to the town limits bothered residents and created health problems until recent times, the memories of which are alive with the author.

Demand grew to sell the surfeit of animal and other locally produced food products. As a way to limit and regulate "peddling or hawking" sales of produce for health reasons, in late 1839 Thibodaux built a structure for a public marketplace. Prior to that time, much of the selling of food occurred informally at different locations and times and through peddlers with carts who moved about the streets. They often could be found at odd and inconvenient hours, loudly hawking their wares. Situated between the courthouse square and Bayou Lafourche, the market became a major attraction. Effective November 1, 1840, the council prohibited "articles of marketing, except for milk, butter, and oysters," from being sold "about the streets of the town" until after ten a.m. and would not allow "butcher meat, fish, fowl, or game" to be offered for sale before then other than at the market house. Meat sale stalls were "left to the free use of the publicke," first come, first served, as long as the stall merchants "shall continue to expose meats for sale therein at least" twice weekly. Unless the stall occupants maintained their spaces "in a neat and cleanly condition" as well, they would be denied use of the stalls.[19] Loud, raucous calls of food hawkers must have echoed throughout the village as peddlers made their rounds in the early hours of the day, before the council regulated some of the practice.

The absence of refrigeration combined with poor public control particularly over fresh meat that came from diseased animals prompted additional rules in 1842. Anyone "offering for sale bringing to market in the town of Thibodaux, the meat of any animal [one assumes this included fish, fowl, and reptile] that may have died from the effects of disease or accident, or that may have been killed when in a state of disease" would be subject to "conviction and a fine of not less than $20 or more than $50, plus the cost of prosecution and forfeiture of the meat."[20] In spite of Mississippi River trade in ice cut from northern lakes and rivers having begun in the early part of the century, Thibodaux appears to have lacked a commercial outlet for ice to use in preserving food. The residents may not have enjoyed even a seasonal supply at least until 1845, when the Thibodaux Ice Company was formed. Represented by the physician and former mayor James A. Scudday, the company leased a lot twenty-two feet wide by fifty feet deep on Jackson Street owned by Charles W. Hawley.[21] In August 1853, just before a major outbreak of yellow fever, the ice business of J. T. Daunis, located at the corner of Main and St. Louis streets, optimistically advertised in *The Thibodaux Minerva*: "ICE! ICE!—I take this method of informing my friends and customers that I shall continue to sell ICE during the hot weather, at 10 cents per pound."[22] In an era before the discovery of bacteria, and with little means of food preservation, the inhabitants of Thibodaux were exposed to many and deadly disorders.

CHAPTER THREE

Kees

The Union Bank, George S. Guion, and Leonidas Polk

Into the scene of the settlement of Thibodaux, around 1828, stepped Absalom Kees. The first of our master carpenters to arrive in the vicinity, Kees found a village whose population had increased from only a few dozen in 1820 to about one hundred. As noted in chapter 2, the village suffered from many problems that coincided with an increase in population: drainage, sanitation, waste disposal, and roaming animals, to name a few. They could not be addressed properly until the community's incorporation in 1838. But even so, Thibodaux expanded and began to prosper; by 1830, the newly dug, privately owned canal connected Bayou Lafourche with the upper, navigable portion of Bayou Terrebonne. Sufficiently wide to handle small flatboats and other lesser watercraft, the canal opened the growing Terrebonne countryside to the New Orleans markets. The town and its improvements gave the promise of freedom and prosperity to hard-working American and foreign newcomers alike.

A skilled carpenter and, according to later description, an "engineer,"[1] Absalom Kees had migrated to Natchez, Mississippi, probably in the early 1820s. Born in 1789, Absalom was raised in the mountains of western South Carolina. The family included his father, Captain John Kees Jr.; mother, Mary Allen Kees; and four siblings: three brothers and a sister. Absalom's father fought in the American Revolution, his grave now marked by the Sons of the American Revolution in a secluded, obscure place in mountainous Oconee County, South Carolina. By 1806, Absalom, already a responsible man, showed engineering and carpentry skills. Before John Kees died in 1806 or 1807, he granted Absalom twenty acres of land and a water-powered grain mill situated alongside Mill Creek, a tributary of the Tugaloo River, together with two sorrel horses.[2] Kees worked as the miller and millwright, operating and maintaining the mill. It provided an essential service, mostly grinding the neighbors' Indian corn, or maize, for their food. The experience gave Kees as good training in engineering and carpentry as could be had in that time and place, and Kees gained valuable experience in business management.[3]

Within a year or so of Captain Kees's death, Absalom left home and removed to Madison, Morgan County, Georgia, located east of modern-day Atlanta. While there, between 1809 and August 1811, Kees served as one of four commissioners responsible for maintaining the town springs and preventing people from cutting timber in their vicinity. He bought town lots and no doubt honed his considerable carpentry talents, learning as well how to build and operate a steam-driven cotton gin.[4] At some point Kees married and around 1820 fathered a daughter, Caroline Amelia (or Emeline).[5]

By then, the family resided near Natchez, where Kees commenced working for Major John Minor, a wealthy cotton planter. Minor's politically influential family came from Kentucky in the 1780s, when Natchez was still Spanish territory. Another Kees daughter, Mary Anna (or Allen), named for Absalom's mother, was born in 1828, in Mississippi. (Mary Anna's birth date was recorded in the 1860 Census of the Kees family, then living near Lockport in the Ninth Ward of Lafourche Parish, Louisiana.)[6]

What drew Kees to the Natchez area? The record does not reveal his reasons for the move west, but likely the energetic and ambitious Kees found a better station in life in the booming new state. The Mississippi Territory became a state in 1817; it had grown immensely since 1810, from 31,306 people, of whom 14,706 were enslaved, to 42,176 free whites and 33,272 enslaved people in 1820. Near to fertile lands in both inland Mississippi and Louisiana across the Mississippi River, between 1799 and 1811 the bluff settlement experienced rapid population growth. The Panic of 1819 and resultant economic depression lessened emigration from the East, but migration to Mississippi continued almost nonstop after the end of the War of 1812. Seemingly endless land became available in Alabama and Mississippi to white Americans originating from the Northeast, the upper South, and the Carolinas and Georgia. Natchez's predominantly cotton-based wealth was astounding. Most of its produce was shipped to nearby New Orleans; from there, ginned cotton bales were loaded aboard seagoing vessels and sent to mills in the northern United States and Great Britain.[7]

Absalom Kees used his talents successfully in a variety of tasks for the Minor family. Living and working in the Natchez community, he became familiar with the classically-designed Greek Revival-style of residential and business structures for which the city remains famous and a tourist attraction in modern times. A knowledge of and experience with such varied building types and construction techniques would benefit him. When Kees's employer, John Minor, learned of the profitability of sugarcane agriculture in south Louisiana, he, like so many others in Natchez and elsewhere, determined to avail himself of the opportunities. In 1828 Minor bought land in Terrebonne Parish. He and his manager, James Dinsmore, also a Kentuckian, sent the versatile Kees there, assigning the master carpenter/mechanic to construct the first steam-driven sugar mill in Terrebonne. The complex included a steam sawmill connected to the sugar mill, a boiling house for the cane syrup, carrier tables for the cane, a cane shed, and cabins for the workers. For many years thereafter, the people held there in slavery labored on one of the largest nineteenth-century sugar plantations in Louisiana. Minor's fertile Terrebonne property later became known as Southdown Plantation; it was situated near a small village, Houma, alongside Bayous Terrebonne and Black. Reporting on his still-incomplete work progress in January 1830, Kees had been living in the area for over a year.[8]

In order to reach Terrebonne in 1828, Kees traveled from Natchez by steamboat or flatboat down the Mississippi River to Donaldsonville, where Bayou Lafourche joined the river. He then had to proceed down Bayou Lafourche, disembarking in Thibodaux, from which Kees either rode by horseback or wagon on the dirt path known as the Terrebonne Road southwest into Terrebonne country. No doubt impressed with Thibodaux's promise, in May 1829 he acquired from James Doris two Thibodaux town lots, numbers 101 and 102 on the original 1820 survey plat by the surveyor, Grinage. The Kees property fronted on Bayou Lafourche close to its intersection with the Terrebonne Road. The lots were probably investments, because Kees sold them in 1833. Although employed in Terrebonne in 1830 working on the mills, sheds, and cabins for Minor, Kees wanted to move to the better, busier location on Bayou Lafourche; in March 1832 he used promissory notes to pay $1,000 for a one-arpent-square lot in Thibodaux from John Davidson Smith, father-in-law of Judge George S. Guion of Concordia Parish and Natchez. Originally a portion of farmland owned by Pierre Himmel and bought by Smith in the 1820s, the lot was situated only a short distance above the intersection of Terrebonne Road with Bayou Lafourche. It was separated from the bayou by a "public highway" atop the stream bank. Two months later, Kees bought from Smith a smaller lot, apparently for a residence and carpentry shop. Situated facing the first block of Terrebonne Road from Bayou Lafourche, it backed up to his property acquired in March. Kees eventually gained prominent neighbors, among them the industrialists Charles W. Hawley and John Larkin. On the larger lot fronting Bayou Lafourche, Kees built a steam-driven sawmill, the first in the area. Logs arrived there from different directions hauled on sledges or in wagons or boated or floated on Bayou Lafourche directly to the bayou bank in front of the sawmill. Now solidly in business in Thibodaux, Kees had a facility that allowed him to profit not only through direct sales of lumber to builders and landowners but from the use of the mill in his own carpentry pursuits. In addition, because Kees's land holdings adjoined the highly-priced commercial/industrial growth area of the town, he, too, benefited from the increased value of his own holdings.[9]

The evidence of a master builder's activity in Lafourche and other parishes can be found in parish records, where contracts to build may be recorded. For several years the records are silent: Kees was either occupied with the sawmill or his carpentry tasks were small scale; or, if his building contracts were written, they simply went unrecorded. But, in 1839, Kees succeeded in landing what likely was his first major construction job in the village, the Thibodaux branch of the Union Bank of Louisiana. With the main office of the bank located in New Orleans, the Union Bank, much like other newly created state banks at that time, began in the Crescent City and were expanding into country towns like Thibodaux. There, close to promising sugar-growing operations and manufacturing industries, the banks furnished credit to plantation owners, merchants, and foundry owners. A written building agreement between Kees, his two partners, and the Union Bank was recorded in April 1839. The bank would change owners several times over the years, and after the start of the twentieth century the magnificent old building became a residence of the Marquette family, eventually a filling station, and finally an auto parts store before its demolition in the 1970s. The bank site is now a parking lot for the Thibodaux branch of the Lafourche Parish Library.[10]

Before Kees commenced the construction of the bank in 1839, he may have realized that running a sawmill took too much time away from his building trade, or he simply may have needed money. That same year Kees had become involved in a residential construction job lasting until 1842 for Pierre Lefebvre, a New Orleanian then domiciled in Lafourche Parish.[11] Lefebvre owned a plantation twenty miles down Bayou Lafourche on the left descending bank. The job size and time required for Lefebvre, in addition to the anticipated time to attend to the work on the Union Bank branch, no doubt prompted Kees to find a buyer for his sawmill. In 1838, Kees sold the "saw mill, dwelling and other buildings, fixtures, and improvements . . . as well as the engine, instruments, tools . . . belonging to the mill or intended for its use, and also a skiff and a horse and horse cart."[12] The buyers, Arthur M. Foley of Assumption Parish and Joseph R. Niles of Thibodaux, paid Kees $10,000 using notes due at the local Union Bank branch.[13] Coincidentally, the village of Thibodaux only then held its initial election; Kees cast his first votes for council trustees and for mayor.

Foley and Niles immediately expanded the sawmill land, adding a half-arpent the same year they acquired the mill. Foley soon bought out Niles, continuing to operate the sawmill and borrowing $1,800. According to the mortgage, the money was to be spent on "the Steam Sawmill Engine Corn Mill" as well as fixtures, a dwelling house, other outbuildings, and probably changes to allow the mill to plane boards of lumber.[14] Before the mid-1840s, Foley had associated a new partner, the Maine native Sumner Townsend. Townsend quickly became one of Thibodaux's most influential citizens, and his partnership with Foley lasted through the Civil War, when Foley died.[15] Foley's succession auction sale in 1866 included his interest in the "Sawmill lot."[16]

Soon after the sale of his sawmill, Absalom Kees, described as a "carpenter, joiner and cabinet maker," and two masons, Jacob Baker and George Anderson, negotiated with Union Bank of Louisiana officials to build the Union Bank branch "banking house."[17] A large presence in the loan mortgage business in Thibodaux since 1833, the bank evidently commenced operations out of leased space. On July 10, 1836, Leufroy Barras, a prominent judge and notary public in Terrebonne, sold the bank a town block fronting on Jackson Street two blocks from Bayou Lafourche for $950. It was bounded by St. Bridget Street (West Fifth today) on the south, Focus Street on the east, and Thibodaux Street (West Fourth) on the north. According to a referenced plan, a town plat, and proposals from the three artisans, who in effect also were contractors, the new bank was to be designed in the Greek Revival style. The contractors were obligated to obtain and have "on the spot . . . the bricks, timber, zinc, Slate, glass, scantling, marble, hardware, paint and other materials" to complete the job. As well, the builders must supply all the workers of different trades "employed by themselves or skilful [*sic*] workmen or

Images 6 and 7. Union Bank of Louisiana building, Jackson Street, Thibodaux (*above*) c. 1895 and (*below*) c. 1950. Courtesy of Nicholls State University Archives.

artists under them." Knowing that not everything could be covered in their agreement, the parties assented to building plan alterations, such as in the placement of a vault, the windows, or other openings in walls. The contractors agreed to receive a total of $8,000.00 for the work and to be paid one-third with the signing of the contract; the remainder was due them when the bank was completed and "delivered key in hand to the cashier of said Branch bank." The remuneration in today's money is estimated as of this writing at more than $240,000, then quite a handsome sum. Of consequence, too, Judge George Seth Guion, of close by Ridgefield Plantation, gave his signature to the contract, among a veritable gallery of other major leaders from around the Lafourche and Terrebonne area: John Mills, Lemuel Tanner, Van P. Winder, P. Marchais, John C. Beatty (or Beattie), Antoine Laforest, and Judge Henry P. Knobloch.

George S. Guion was one of the more prominent citizens of Thibodaux in 1839 and arguably the most significant of Kees's local contacts in his early career in Thibodaux. As noted previously, Guion's wife, Caroline Winder, was the stepdaughter of John Davidson Smith, the owner of the three-arpent-wide tract of land that Smith bought from Pierre Himmel. At Smith's death in 1832, Caroline inherited the Smith plantation, named Ridgefield. Given control and management of Ridgefield, her husband quickly assumed a leadership role in Thibodaux and continued subdividing the Ridgefield Plantation property that Smith had commenced on the west side of Jackson Street. Kees, who at the time still owned the sawmill near the Guion lands and downtown, and Guion both had ties with the Natchez community from which Kees emigrated; Kees, active in the Lafourche region building trade, knew the Guions well. It was helpful to Guion, too, that Kees was versed in the Greek Revival architectural styles that Natchez so prominently displayed. Absalom Kees was the right man for the important job of constructing Thibodaux's first large bank building.[18]

Along with his work on the Union Bank branch, Kees participated in local Thibodaux politics. He ran for—and with twenty-nine votes won—a trustee seat on the village's council in May 1839. His election gives us additional evidence not only of his involvement in the community but of the respect he had gained from the voters. For most of the master builders about whom this work is written, their political connections and personal political involvement were crucial to their professional careers in and around Thibodaux. Kees served as a trustee for one year, followed by a gap in his political activity, perhaps due to his having moved outside the village boundary or to the press of work elsewhere. Kees ran again in 1846; he won a trustee position with twenty-seven votes.[19]

Two other out-of-state builders arrived in Thibodaux in 1840 and influenced Kees's fortunes. James Frost and a friend, Morgan Springer, came from Uniontown, in western Pennsylvania. The area featured rich farmlands, hills and valleys, and low mountains; among that landscape still stand numerous eighteenth- and nineteenth-century solid brick and limestone houses, barns, inns, and taverns. Their constructions required skilled craftsmen. Many of the structures lie alongside the famed National Road, now US Route 40. Nearby, the city of Brownsville sits on the Monongahela River. There, Frost and Springer had opportunities to broaden their skills. Steamboats and flatboats were built to work the Ohio and Mississippi Rivers and their tributaries and distributaries like Bayou Lafourche. Before leaving to seek their fortunes in Louisiana, the two young carpenters received a solid training in building trades using wood, brick, and stone materials.[20] After their arrival, both men quickly associated with Kees, and Frost and Kees became co-builders in 1843–1844 in the construction of St. John's, one of Louisiana's most historic and beautiful Protestant Episcopal churches.

IMAGE 8. Josiah Frost House, near Uniontown, Fayette County, Pennsylvania. Josiah Frost was the father of James Frost. Public domain, courtesy of Wikimedia Commons.

A prestigious American arrived on the Lafourche around the same time, 1841 to 1842: Leonidas Polk, an Episcopal minister in Tennessee and cousin to Senator James K. Polk, had recently been appointed as Episcopal bishop of Louisiana. Polk and his wife Frances Devereux moved from Ashwood Hall near Columbia, Tennessee, to live at Leighton Plantation, two miles up Bayou Lafourche from the Guion residence at Ridgefield. The Polks operated Leighton as a large sugarcane plantation worked by enslaved people and containing a mill to crush the sugarcane and process the juice. Polk became a close friend of Guion and of other Protestant migrants to the community. The early conditions in Thibodaux for formal Christian worship were considered to be disorganized, if not disgraceful, by both Polk and Reverend Charles Menard, the new Roman Catholic priest. Almost immediately after Bishop Polk and his family made their appearance in 1842, he established an Episcopal congregation. Its local church founders included medical and legal professionals, manufacturers, merchants, and planters, all men of substance and influence, some of them Methodists or Presbyterians. By 1843, George S. and Caroline Winder Guion reserved an entire surveyed town block of their Ridgefield land for the church and cemetery, and the church building committee stood ready to construct St. John's Episcopal Church. It would front on Jackson Street not far down from the more settled areas of the town.[21]

A graduate of the United States Military Academy at West Point, New York, Bishop Polk knew design principles. He planned and had his Tennessee residence, Ashwood Hall, built in the Greek Revival mode, and he designed and helped build St. John's Episcopal Church near Columbia, Tennessee, in the same style. Polk was experienced in construction and engineering. He was also familiar with the large and elaborately designed Greek Revival-styled Episcopal cathedral, Christ Church, on Canal Street in New Orleans, dating to 1837. Thus inspired to use Greek Revival, and specifically Doric temple style, for St. John's in Thibodaux, Polk created plans for the church. He was assisted by Charles Hawley, the experienced engineer and foundryman, in designing the church's old-fashioned box seating arrangement. Guion's work with Absalom Kees on the Union Bank and Kees's bonds over the prior decade with other church founders no doubt prompted the building committee of St. John's to choose Kees as the primary builder.

The contract to construct St. John's included not just Kees but James Frost. The background story involves the aforementioned Pierre Lefebvre of New Orleans. In 1818 Lefebvre had acquired his large Bayou Lafourche tract from the famed politician and diplomat Edward Livingston. Lefebvre began work on his residence and other buildings on the Bayou Lafourche land in 1839, using Kees as the builder. We know, as well, that when Springer and Frost appeared in Thibodaux in late 1840, Kees hired both for the large Lefebvre job on the bayou twenty miles down from Thibodaux. Kees needed good carpenters to help construct Lefebvre's improvements. An existing manuscript account of Lefebvre shows that among almost $600 of charges that Kees incurred were for materials ordered from New Orleans for Frost and Springer in April 1841. It is likely that Kees befriended Frost, a fellow Methodist, and wanted to bring the youth into the business arena in Thibodaux. Introducing Frost to the community by means of the St. John's work would provide the younger man with opportunity for a broad range of work. Moreover, Kees knew that, in building St. John's in Thibodaux, much of his time and effort must be spent at his shop preparing the lumber for the church and in managing a large group of laborers. He required someone with experience to handle daily supervision on the jobsite. Finally, the work on St. John's demanded a thorough understanding of masonry construction. The specialty probably was not one in which Kees had sufficient experience, judging by the Union Bank branch effort; there, Kees had the title of "carpenter and joiner" and the two other partners that of "masons."[22] Frost came from a region where brick and stone construction prevailed; his familiarity with and expertise in such a trade, in addition to carpentry and joinery, filled the needs of St. John's in the joint effort of Absalom Kees and James Frost.[23]

Considerable endeavor went into the formalities of developing and writing the St. John's contract. It appears to have been a joint effort between Bishop Polk, the building committee of St. John's, and the two master builders. Very likely, the work on the new Episcopal church already had begun before the contract was signed on September 28, 1843. St. John's would take fully eight months to complete. By the time the work ended, Kees had become involved in other town-based projects.

CHAPTER FOUR

Kees and Frost

St. John's, the First Methodist Church, and a Residence for Madame Thibodaux

The St. John's building contract was recorded on September 28, 1843, soon after its signing. Between then and January 1, 1844, Kees and Frost completed St. John's Episcopal Church. That, at least, is the impression given by Bishop Leonidas Polk, who, as a founder and the church's architect, kept close tabs on the construction. Speaking to the Louisiana Diocesan Convention in June 1844, the bishop declared his having "laid . . . the cornerstone of a remarkably neat church in the village of Thibodaux" on New Year's Day, 1844.[1] After only three months underway, could it have been so complete as to elicit the term "remarkably neat church"?

Indeed, finishing the church was longer in the making. Bishop Polk's address to the convention included claims that the building was "nearly ready for consecration," and that the congregation "will, within a few months of its inception, have carried out their plan" to build the church.[2] The "plan" had been born at least by early summer 1843, because on July 20 an advertisement appeared in the New Orleans *Daily Picayune* stating that the New Orleans-based commission firm of Laforest & Squires, located at 20 Old Levee Road, sought "sealed proposals" for the construction of the church and had available for inspection "a plan of the church, with particulars."[3] The building contract itself provided for the expected time of completion as May 1, 1844. At the very least, expectations governed payment for the church's completion, the contract noting that "no portion of said balance [of contracted money] can be claimed as due before the first day of March next," meaning March 1, 1844.[4] Finally, the consecration of Reverend David Kerr, the first priest at St. John's, did not occur until a year later. St. John's did not receive the finishing touches until at least April or May 1844; it was unprepared for business in early January 1844.

Polk's plan called for a Greek Revival-style temple based upon schemes set forth in *The Modern Builder's Guide*, a carpenter's handbook first published in 1833.[5] Written by a New York builder/architect named Minard Lafever, the instruction book (and other published builder guides) immensely influenced construction art in America during the first half of the nineteenth century. Given the lack of trained architects in the United States, all people working in the building trades found such manuals to be requisites in the complex challenges of designing banks, churches, and homes. Even barns and sheds, outdoor kitchens, and privies (or necessaries) were occasionally built in Greek Revival, Gothic Revival, and other styles explained and illustrated in detail in printed builder guides. And, as one might anticipate, the builders/artisans who undertook the daily construction of buildings had a strong influence on the design details of their creations. They were architects as well as builders and contractors.

The agreement between the St. John's building committee and the master builders, Kees and Frost, called for "a front [width] of thirty-six feet from out to out, by a length of sixty feet including a gallery, a portico of twelve feet in depth on the front of said building."[6] Massive brick walls eighteen inches thick lofted twenty-five feet high. Originally specified for "cypress shingles," the roof ended up being constituted of heavy slate. The roof framing required that it support a future cupola above the pediment that topped the four outer gallery columns, each column to be "finished on the doric Order [*sic*]." Three tall windows, all still in use for daylighting, graced each side of the church; all windows to have what became known as a Greek key molding in the same style used for the doorway frames. The interior walls received three coats of plaster and paint, but the building contract specified that the exterior brick walls were to be painted to resemble stone. As an indication that almost everything used in construction was from the area, the contractors were responsible to furnish all the materials, which must be "as of good quality as can be obtained in the neighborhood." That requirement could not always be met. Sand for masonry work, for example, may have come from Mississippi. In 1845, Kees paid $100 to Christopher Bougher of Vicksburg for "a load of sand,"[7] which Bougher transported to Thibodaux by flatboat. In addition, the slate roof was unavailable locally but probably originated at a quarry in the northern United States or even Wales in Great Britain. The evidence is lacking, but some of the bricks required for the church walls at St. John's may have been made by enslaved crews using clay from the soils in the church plot.[8]

For the recently incorporated village of Thibodaux, St. John's constituted an immense structure. Its size and complexity unrivaled except for the Union Bank branch, St. John's helped seal the reputation of Absalom Kees as a skilled artisan and gave James Frost a solid start in the community.

How did Kees and Frost accomplish their work? Describing its progress involves some speculation, because there is no day-by-day record of what happened or exactly when. But site work for St. John's began as early as July or August 1843. Surveying the site, trenching for the foundations, and infilling soil commenced the operations. The official building contract recording on September 23 surely occurred weeks after its signing, or at least after reaching a preliminary agreement.

Local enslaved labor was available for lease from several of the nearby church organizers, like the industrialist and town trustee Charles Hawley,[9] and especially from the Guions on Ridgefield Plantation. Perhaps other members of the building committee or Bishop Polk supplied some laborers. Leasing trained artisans and even untrained enslaved labor was common in the antebellum South. Once the harvest and grinding of sugarcane began in early to mid-October, however, most of the plantation-based laborers could not be spared. And although Frost had not yet officially bought an enslaved man, Kees then owned at least four, including three craftsmen named Jake, Ben, and Thornton.[10] All were skilled in specialties of the building trade and highly valued. The fourth person, named Nathan, had been bought in 1842 from William Tabor Sr. by Kees for $400. Then only fourteen, Nathan was resold in 1847 to his mother, a free woman of color named Rachel Tabor. Rachel also paid Kees $400.[11]

Enslaved people were forced to work at St. John's in wide-ranging construction roles. Many undertook the heavy labor of digging the trenches for the wide-based, pyramid-laid brick foundations for the walls. Others, like carpenters, assisted in the roof framing, joinery, and finishing accomplished on the site as well as in one of the carpenter shops. And enslaved masons capably set and mortared the thousands of locally-made bricks used in the church walls. The existence of St. John's and many other structures in early Thibodaux was as much owing to the strength, skills, and perseverance of enslaved men as to the contracted white builders. In their renowned biography, *Henry Howard: Louisiana's Architect*, authors Robert Brantley and Victor McGee claim that legal documents indicate "most of the skilled [construction] work preceding the Civil War was performed by contracted free laborers, largely Irish and German immigrants."[12] Their assertion does not match the findings in this book for the Bayou Lafourche scene.

Another question that should be addressed is what part free people of color might have played in the Thibodaux building trades. Unlike their major role in building New Orleans dating back before 1800, there does not appear to have been a similar use for or even a noticeable presence of free Black laborers in the antebellum bayou region of Lafourche. Insofar as the overall labor situation played out in the locale, both free white and enslaved Black artisans contributed their skills in constructing a variety of homes, commercial structures, factories, schools, churches, and government buildings. Since statehood, the area had developed as a part of the dominant plantation culture, quite in contrast to antebellum New Orleans in what it offered for artisan labor.

The lack of a daily record of the building of St. John's in 1843–1844 is regrettable, but one may easily imagine the work panorama. Dawn brought forth the crews, who arrived at the site on foot or with ox- or horse-drawn carts. Employing carts for transport was described in 1874 (and again in 1890) by Silas Grisamore, who migrated in the late 1840s to the Lafourche from Indiana: each cart was "pushed" by a pair of oxen tied together by the horns and guided in front by a man or boy on a horse hitched to the cart tongue and another in the cart with a long pole to poke a laggard ox. Built entirely of wood and having no grease, in Grisamore's memory the cart wheels and axles made "such an infernal screeching that they could be heard three miles, and, the yelling of the drivers, loud enough to be heard above that."[13] Kees and Frost both came from nearby homes and shops bringing water kegs, tool chests, lumber, framing, moldings, and whatever else the day's needs might be. The materials might be carried in wagons or carts in dry weather, or in muddy conditions probably by ox- or horse-drawn sledges, which slid on the ground using runners. Among the number of men making their way to the workplace, enslaved workers appeared from their sleeping quarters, some in the town, others brought from plantations, where they were usually awakened by bells. Those from the adjacent Ridgefield Plantation were returned there nightly, but other leased plantation laborers may have been housed temporarily in the village.[14]

Late summer and early autumn weather in south Louisiana may be dry, allowing construction of the outer parts of the building to proceed routinely until more climatologically iffy November; by then, a roof probably covered the unfinished church. The site must have been as busy as any the village had seen. So much required to be erected, or laid down, joined together with mortises and held by iron nails or wooden pegs, plastered, painted, and, as the contract specified, "the portico laid with brick to imitate stone," the metal chimney erected, and a furnace installed—all to be done in such a short time.[15]

Once a quiet place away from the town center, the construction site during that fall, winter, and early spring of 1843–1844 reverberated with hammering, sawing, and chiseling, and the songs or yells of workers. Like other undeveloped areas of Thibodaux, the western corner of Jackson and Cider (now West Seventh) Streets resembled a cleared place in a swampy forest, although St. John's had neighbors. The home of Francois Brunet lay diagonally across on the corner of Jackson and Cider Street, and Thomas Hargis and Isaac Corbit owned two half-lots directly across fronting on Jackson. A few other lots along the east side of Jackson had been sold by Mrs. Thibodaux in the 1830s and contained residences. Charles Hawley built his residence on the half-lot across Jackson from the church, which he acquired from Mrs. Thibodaux in 1836 for $250. When purchased, his half-lot was surrounded on all sides by vacant lots, but by the time Hawley sold Thomas Hargis his home (referenced as "all buildings") and lot in 1839, he had neighbors Francois Brunet across on the opposite (east) corner of Cider Street, and Isaac Corbit beside him on the other half-lot facing Jackson. Behind or east of Hargis and Corbit, Mrs. Thibodaux still owned the timbered vacant lots. The neighborhood of early St. John's Episcopal Church thus appears to have been partially settled, mainly along Jackson, leaving some still-empty, forested lots going east toward the canal.[16]

The large town block set aside by the Guions for St. John's was rough pasture dotted with scrubby trees, as well as dwarf palmetto, of which many are still found in the live-oak-lined perimeter of the historic cemetery. A variety of smells, familiar to the workers but surely not to us in our time, impregnated the air: animals frequently had free roam, left their markings, died, and rotted in place. Jackson Street was a dust storm when dry, as ox carts and horse-drawn buggies passed and the wind blew. It remained a rutted, muddy path after rains.

On June 18, 1844, Kees signed another contract for a Methodist Episcopal church to be constructed on a half-lot only a block up the street, at the corner of Jackson and St. Mary.[17] The new agreement was additional indication that he and Frost had finished the work on St. John's. The land had been granted to the trustees of the Methodist Episcopal Church of Thibodaux.[18] In contrast with the elaborate St. John's Episcopal Church, which cost more than $5,000, Kees built the wood-frame Methodist Episcopal church for only $1,200. The agreement between him and the two committeemen, James Billiu of Lafourche and Francis Mead of Terrebonne, specified an edifice of only thirty by forty feet. Yet it, too, was to be in the Greek Revival style: "A portico of neat workmanship shall be erected and attached to the front . . . ten feet wide upon four columns either square or turned at the option of the builder."[19] Like St. John's, the portico was topped by a pediment and side and raking cornices, but the design did not contemplate a cupola or steeple. The plans called for a plain and simple structure, without an altar and kneeling bench and adorned only with a pulpit. Aside from front and side elevation drawings and a floor plan, Kees was left to design and build, independent of the committee, what appears to have

IMAGE 9. Architectural drawing, probably sketched by Absalom Kees, of the First Methodist Church in Thibodaux. Courtesy of Nicholls State University Archives.

been his own congregation's church. Directed to complete the church by the following November 1 and paid $275 down, Kees obtained permission to receive additional advances as needed.

Absalom Kees's local accomplishments to 1845 were notable: property owner; builder of Terrebonne Parish's first steam sugar and sawmills; builder, owner, and operator of Thibodaux's first steam sawmill; builder of the major regional bank branch of the Union Bank of Louisiana; builder of the first Episcopal church west of the Mississippi River; and designer and builder of the original Methodist church in Thibodaux. He had served as a trustee on the village council in 1839, soon after Thibodaux's incorporation, and he was elected again for two years beginning May 1846. Kees's latter term on the council coincided with a major Thibodaux construction project that rivaled even St. John's in size and difficulty. It began in June 1845 and was not completed until September 1847.

In the central part of Thibodaux lay two lots, considered to be one large lot numbered 10 on the James Grinage survey. It was owned mainly by Brigitte Belanger Thibodaux, who for almost twenty years had been a civic leader and town developer. The property was bounded on the north by Levee Street (with Bayou Lafourche flowing just in front of it), Maronge Street to the east, Green Street to the west, and Market Street on the south side, separating lot 10 from the courthouse square. A portion of the lot already contained the market house, used by residents to sell and buy fresh vegetables and animal and fish products. In June 1845, Madame Thibodaux determined to construct two large buildings on her lot, a place that now contains Thibodaux City Hall and adjoining parking lots. A son, Henry Claiborne Thibodaux, acted as her agent to contract with Kees to build both structures. Kees would be occupied on the job for more than two years, when he acknowledged having been fully paid the $8,800 for which he was contracted, plus $572.33 "for extra work." Kees's hand-drawn images of the plans survived and are preserved in the Nicholls State University Archives in Thibodaux.[20]

As described in a payment acknowledgment recorded in September 1847, Kees created "a two-story brick building and a brick warehouse." One structure served partly as a residence, perhaps for Brigitte Thibodaux; five rooms were built on its second floor, each room having a fireplace and coal-burning grate. The three front rooms were separated from two in the rear by a hallway. Six rooms were located on the ground floor, three of which served as storerooms; "a bedroom & counting room back of and adjoining each [storeroom]"[21] took up the rest of the ground floor complex. A two-story L-wing of brick extended off and to the rear of the main structure. It contained two ground-level rooms for the kitchen and four rooms above, presumably bedrooms for staff and/or dining rooms. The wing connected to the main house by a covered gallery. The main structure extended fifty-six feet along Levee Street by a depth of fifty feet. Behind the mixed-use building, close to Market Street, Kees was obligated to build the brick warehouse, thirty-five feet wide and elevated two and one-half feet.

None of the residential and warehouse structures or the adjacent market house exists today. Writing in 1890, *The Weekly Thibodaux Sentinel* editor Silas Grisamore related that the market house, in which the top floor contained the Thibodaux council meeting room, burned in 1861 or 1862 due to sparks from a steamboat in the bayou. Later rebuilt and centered between Green and Maronge Streets on lot 10, the new market house remained at the time the first Sanborn fire insurance maps were created in 1885. None of the two structures that Kees built for Madame Thibodaux was shown on that 1885 map. Although their fates are unknown, they may have succumbed to the same fire that destroyed the original market house.[22]

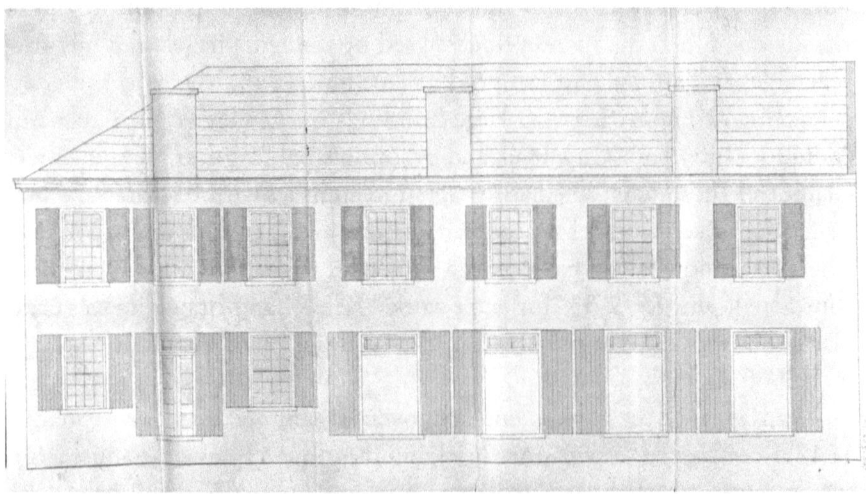

IMAGE 10. Front elevation of Brigitte Bellanger Thibodaux's market square building signed "A. Kees, 1845." Courtesy of Nicholls State University Archives.

When Kees completed his work, the lot in front of the Lafourche Parish courthouse between Green and Maronge Streets contained arguably the finest brick structures in town. His attention may have been directed then to Houma, where, in October 1846, he was authorized by the Terrebonne Parish Police Jury to build "an office for the Parish of Terrebonne Recorder Clerk and Sheriff."[23] But by March 1847, Kees seems to have decided to make some changes in his life and reduce his building trade activities. At the age of fifty-eight, Absalom Kees commenced selling several of his valuable enslaved artisans, including one to his master builder friend James Frost. Another sale concerned Nathan, enslaved son of Rachel, a free woman of color.[24] Her will, drafted in January 1848, directed that Nathan be purchased from his owner, Absalom Kees, manumitted, and set free.[25] The will had been dictated to Judge Gustavus A. Knobloch and witnessed by Kees, George Anderson (a mason on the Union Bank of Louisiana job in 1839), James Jennings, and Victor Richard. In 1850, Kees emancipated an enslaved woman named Celia, age fifty, in recognition of her long and faithful service as a domestic, with a promise that Kees would maintain her during her life should she become unable to manage affairs.[26] In September 1852, Kees emancipated another woman, age twenty-eight, also named Rachel, and her son James, age "6 or 8," the act promising that they "shall be and remain in the State of Louisiana enjoying all the rights and privileges to which by law free persons of color residing in the State of Louisiana are entitled to."[27] In spite of these acts of charity, Kees continued to hold others in servitude; the Census of 1850 recorded Kees still in Thibodaux and owner of eleven enslaved persons, of whom two were adult females (probably the aforementioned Celia and Rachel), and three unnamed children.[28]

Then sixty-one years old, Kees lived alone in the census-designated Thibodaux household 420, near three other carpenters including Morgan Springer. All were located on the west side of Jackson Street. Kees's residence in 1850 may have been different from his original home, because in March 1848 he sold his home and shop above Jackson Street fronting on the public road alongside Bayou Lafourche to Owen Conlan.[29] Perhaps Kees was leasing a habitation when the census was taken. In 1851, before retiring fully, Kees agreed to assist the Methodist church in an extensive renovation. A number of listed items in the "Specifications of work to be done" required the work "to be finished similar in material and workmanship to the Episcopal Church in Thibodaux."[30] It was a sign that the original Methodist church structure had not served the aesthetic or quality expectations of the church fathers. Kees contracted to complete the work by March 1852, at which time he leased another town lot, about the size of half a city block and situated a few blocks east of his old residence, bounded in front or north by St. Bridget (now East Fifth) Street and on the east and west sides by Green and St. Louis Streets. Kees agreed to repair the houses on the lot, which was owned in absentia by Philip A. Sergeant.[31] After only four months, in late July 1852, Kees again transacted for land, this time a short distance into rural Terrebonne Parish. He paid $750 to George Milroy for a half-interest in property of one and a quarter arpents frontage on Bayou Terrebonne and twenty arpents depth; a few months later, he acquired the other half-interest. The tract was bounded below by the Ducros Plantation of Van P. Winder and above (toward Thibodaux) by Theodile Malbrough. No evidence of the rural land having been resold has been found in Lafourche and Terrebonne Parish records.[32]

Absalom Kees's finally grappled with his move down Bayou Lafourche and away from the Thibodaux area. A major shift away from his longtime association with the town and with life there, the relocation may have been occasioned partly by a desire to enter into what he perceived as the more profitable and socially-elevated occupation of sugar planting and manufacturing. The risks to life in the aftermath of the 1853 yellow fever epidemic surely helped persuade Kees to leave the populous northern part of Lafourche Parish at this time. The mosquito-borne virus, introduced by railroad workers returning to the Lafourche region after summertime weekends in the already infected city of New Orleans, decimated the town and country populations along and near the bayou above Lafourche Crossing until the late fall. In addition, his daughters Emily (or Emeline) and Mary had married and had children. (Mary was by then a widow of George Davis.) A widower for many years but close to the daughters and their families, Kees had an interest in the children's welfare and safety.

Kees resettled in December 1853, when he bought for $1,900 an undivided half-interest in the Sawmill Plantation, a large tract of land near Lockport, twenty-two miles down Bayou Lafourche. The property, which backed up to a large, shallow body of water situated between Bayous Lafourche and Terrebonne and known as Lake Fields, measured forty arpents front on the right-descending bank of Bayou Lafourche by forty arpents in depth. The seller, Wayne Tanner, owned the land together with his brother

Robert. The parties' sales agreement obligated Kees to pay installments of $625, each due in March 1854 and March 1855, as well as to fulfill the task, worth the $1,250 balance due, of reconstructing a flood-damaged levee in front of the property. Before having to pay the second installment, however, his co-owner Robert Tanner died, and Kees paid $1,250 to Robert Tanner's succession for the other half-interest in the plantation. As of February 1, 1855, Absalom Kees was sole owner of a sizable plantation on Bayou Lafourche, just above the village of Lockport.[33]

Even earlier, in 1853, Kees had begun the levee repairs near Lockport, hiring a contractor and making a partial payment by note. A dispute arose with Kees's contractor, whom Kees accused of unsatisfactory work.[34] Between his Sawmill Plantation property acquisition and 1856, Kees sold from the plantation six parcels of varying widths, totaling twenty-five and a half arpents front, to nearby property owners. He thus owned fourteen and a half arpents by forty arpents of the original Sawmill Plantation lands. The sales brought Kees $7,000, a substantial profit over the $3,150 he paid for the entire forty-arpent-square Sawmill Plantation a short time earlier.[35]

When the 1860 Census was taken, the Kees family resided on their plantation in the Ninth Ward of Lafourche Parish. Kees had reached the age of seventy, his land was valued at $10,000, and he held five people in slavery ("personal property") valued at $7,000. His daughter Emeline and her Prussian-born husband, Edward Meegel, both age forty, had their son, Robert, only eight. He and one Frederick Meegel, also a native of Prussia, age twenty-eight and evidently Edward's brother, were included in the household. Additionally living with Kees were his younger daughter, Mary Davis, and her two children, Frederick, age fifteen, and Charles, age twelve.[36] Within a year of the census taking, on January 8, 1861, Kees sold to Frederick Meegel another parcel of the plantation, nine arpents wide on Bayou Lafourche by forty arpents in depth, for $3,600 cash.[37]

Kees's departure from the Thibodaux scene must have been a shock to his friends and associates. A major player in the business, political life, and building trade of the area for many years, Kees showed qualities that Alexis de Tocqueville saw in American society overall: a love of commerce and the "audacity and the greatness of their industrial undertakings."[38] Thankfully, Kees was replaced in Thibodaux by his able friends Morgan Springer and, until his death in late 1853, James A. Frost. They were numbered among other master carpenters, including Edward T. Burnham of Connecticut,

Sciotha S. Evans, from Missouri, and John Bellsen, originally from New York and living in Assumption Parish. Gifted artisans all, they combined to remake the small town of Thibodaux into one of Louisiana's most desirable and active centers of government, commerce, and residential life in the antebellum era.

CHAPTER FIVE

Frost and Springer
The Two Pennsylvanians

In the western part of Pennsylvania, Fayette County is a long-settled region of lovely mountains and valleys positioned near the Monongahela River. Pioneers from the Eastern Seaboard of continental America began to arrive in the area soon after the French and Indian War. Among them were two New Jersey families named Frost and Springer. Two descendants of those migrants, Morgan Springer and James Aaron Frost, both born in Fayette County, left Pennsylvania in 1840. Their destination was Thibodaux, in a part of the old Mississippi River Delta of southeastern Louisiana sometimes known as the Valley of the Lafourche.

James Aaron (or Allen) Frost was born in 1811 to Josiah Frost and Polly Caulley and grew up in Fayette County, of which Uniontown became the county seat.[1] By then, members of the Frost family had resided around Uniontown for several generations. James Aaron Frost's father settled in Menallen Township, near Uniontown. His home was alongside the National Road, a major east-west route built after the War of 1812 atop a well-worn wagon road that had existed since the French and Indian War. The roadway began in Baltimore and eventually extended to Indiana.

In time replaced by US Route 40, the National Road readily enabled land-hungry settlers to connect to the Ohio and Mississippi Rivers on their way to the "Old Southwest" and other areas west of the Alleghenies throughout the latter part of the eighteenth and first half of the nineteenth century. Conversely, western-located settlers had access via the National Road to markets in the eastern part of the new nation. The National Road additionally encouraged business ventures to locate alongside and serve travelers' needs. Among the entrepreneurs to establish a new business was Josiah Frost. Between 1816 and 1819, he acquired 113 acres and built a stone dwelling house on one side of the road and a tavern and inn opposite. Frost's site drew other commercial concerns, among them a blacksmith shop, saddlery, general store, and post office. The compound became known as Searight's

Corners, for William Searight, to whom in 1821 Frost sold his tavern, other buildings, and the land.[2]

Josiah's son James Aaron Frost brought with him a neighbor and companion on the float south to Thibodaux: Morgan Springer, born in 1814 in Fayette County. His father Zadock was born in 1770, also in Fayette County, but Morgan's mother Eleanor McIntyre was born in Ohio County, Virginia (now West Virginia), in 1776, not far from Uniontown. Morgan's family roots stretch to Burlington County, New Jersey, where his great-grandfather Dennis Springer lived and where Morgan's grandfather Levi Springer was born. In 1760 the Springer family resettled to the Virginia frontier community of Apple Pie Ridge, in Frederick County. They moved again around 1769 north to Fayette County, Pennsylvania.[3]

Of almost certain significance for the story of Morgan Springer is that one of Morgan's uncles, Levi Jr., entered into the occupation of a boatman. His work involved traveling by flatboat from the boatbuilding center of Brownsville on the Monongahela River to New Orleans, then returning to Pennsylvania by horseback from Natchez using the Natchez Trace, or alternatively by sailing vessel to reach New York City. By the time that the National Road passed through Fayette County, Levi Springer Jr. had become a farmer and tavern owner.[4] His earlier travels to Louisiana and back would have been part of the lore of family gatherings and assisted Morgan Springer when he, too, boated downriver years later.

Morgan Springer's father engaged in local politics as a justice of the peace between 1803 and 1818,[5] and he joined a friend, James Allen, to found Fayette County's second newspaper, *The Genius of Liberty and Fayette Advertiser*. Allen and Springer published the newspaper only until 1807, when one Jesse Beeson took charge and ran it until 1818.[6] Morgan Springer and his brother, Dennis J. Springer (1817–1886), evidently were raised by at least one literate parent.

As a youth, Morgan Springer also benefited from having no less than two close relatives in the building trade; he no doubt worked for them and learned the various associated crafts. One of those kin was another uncle, also Dennis Springer, a son of Levi Springer Sr. (The first name Dennis is repeated throughout the family in the eighteenth and nineteenth centuries.) This Dennis Springer became a building contractor and constructed the first Fayette County courthouse in Uniontown in 1776; his farm made the bricks.[7] In 1796 he removed the courthouse and built a new one, receiving

$1,362.53 from the county for his work. Stone and brick materials proliferated in the construction of barns, taverns, dwellings, and other structures in Fayette and adjoining areas when Morgan was a youth. In 1817, Morgan's one-time boatman uncle, Levi Springer Jr., erected a large, solid brick and stone home serving also as a stage hotel for travelers on the new National Road.[8] It stood until 2015, when vandals set fire to the then-vacant mansion. The house and its outbuildings had been listed on the National Register of Historic Places in 1982.[9]

This background information suggests that the two Uniontown, Pennsylvania, migrants to Louisiana's Lafourche countryside in 1840 originated from solid, prospering, literate families. The youths had taken up building trades well before they departed for Louisiana. Perhaps Levi Springer Jr., the boatman, inspired them to seek new lives in the Deep South. But why would they have chosen Thibodaux? They likely arrived in 1840 during the late fall or early winter, a time of year when the Ohio and Mississippi River flatboats, steamboats, and barges carried Midwestern flour, whiskey, meat, and newly harvested apples, corn, and other farm items to Louisiana in exchange for sugar and molasses. Perhaps the two men paid for the trip, or they hired on to assist with the difficult boating tasks. Perhaps they had learned of opportunities in the Lafourche region from their local weekly newspapers. Or even from boatmates en route west and south. We know that they arrived at the very moment when the Bayou Lafourche master builder Absalom Kees had serious work to do, and he needed their help.

According to observations of the nineteenth-century Bayou Lafourche planter William W. Pugh, when Frost and Springer landed, Thibodaux "had no pretensions to be called a commercial center."[10] New Orleans still furnished directly most of the goods required by planters and others, and as Pugh commented, "the village merchants only sold in small quantities to parties who could not send to the city." But that soon changed, and by the end of the 1840s, Thibodaux had become a regional center of trade and manufacturing. Frost and Springer arrived at a propitious time; laborers skilled in the building trades were in demand.

A momentous early and work-unrelated event for James Aaron Frost in Thibodaux was his marriage to Almira Elizabeth Ragan on November 23, 1842. Then age seventeen, Almira was a daughter of James C. Regan of Pennsylvania and Mary B. Conklin of New York. (Mary Conklin Regan changed the name spelling to Ragan after the death of James A. Frost.)

Almira had six siblings, and the Ragans had been part of and prospered in the Thibodaux community since about 1825. Little is known of Almira Ragan Frost, who, before her death in February 1854, had given birth to six children; her and James Aaron Frost's numerous descendants remain in Thibodaux and the surrounds.[11]

The two Pennsylvanians' connection with Absalom Kees began shortly after their arrival on Bayou Lafourche; it occurred so soon that one wonders if Kees awaited the travelers on the bayou bank when they stepped off the boat. As described in chapter three, Frost and Springer almost immediately began working with Kees on the lengthy construction job that Kees had commenced in early 1839 for the wealthy New Orleanian Pierre Lefebvre. The task involved building Lefebvre's "country" residence and other structures some twenty miles down Bayou Lafourche on a large tract that he had bought from Edward Livingston in 1818. Kees needed helpers, and he had them. In an entry on April 11, 1841, the accounts kept for Kees show that materials had been ordered for Frost and Springer, costing $583.56 ¼. Five months later, in August 1841, Kees used notes drawn on Pierre Lefebvre to pay Morgan Springer and James Frost "for work done on" Lefebvre's "house in Lafourche Interior."[12] Springer and Frost were forced to sue Lefebvre to collect on the notes.[13] The work continued into 1842, when Kees too had to sue his employer for money owed. In a Lafourche Parish jury trial that October 15, Kees obtained a sizable judgment of $4,857.46 against Lefebvre.[14]

Kees not only hired the Pennsylvanians upon their arrival in Thibodaux, but he also mentored the new arrivals and introduced them to others who would employ them. During or soon after the Lefebvre stint, Kees no doubt presented James Frost to George S. Guion. The Guion contacts with both Kees and Frost surely led to Frost's association with Kees on the new St. John's Episcopal Church, in the founding of which Guion had such a role. In addition, even before the St. John's work began, in February 1843 Frost and Springer simultaneously acquired from Guion adjacent lots fronting along Jackson Street between St. Mary Street and West Seventh Street (then called Cider Street). Frost's corner lot, number 154 on the 1842 Grinage map, was bought for $450. It was bounded on the north by St. Mary Street and on the south by Lot 155, which Springer bought for $400. Both men received releases of their mortgages in 1845, following timely payments in 1844 of the balances owed to Guion. Frost, however, attracted by an offer for the lot at a much higher price than he paid, sold his corner lot in late 1845 to

Thomas Walton for $1,200. Shortly thereafter, it was sold again for the same price to Sumner Townsend, Charles Yates, and Arthur M. Foley, Methodist elders representing the church congregation. The former property of James Frost thereby became the site for the new church, known as First Methodist Church of Thibodaux, of which Absalom Kees was the builder.[15]

Following the completion of St. John's in 1844, Frost and Springer created their own partnership. In need of a site for their carpentry business, in 1847 they purchased several parcels near the corner of St. Mary and Jackson, close to Kees, from John Larkin, Dr. Thomas M. Williams, and Charles Hawley. Around this time, Larkin, a foundry owner, hired Frost and Springer to construct a prominent brick house fronting on Jackson Street. The building contract in Lafourche Parish records gives us a rare illustration of a well-built, center-of-town, mixed-use, two-story brick house in 1840s Thibodaux.[16]

IMAGE 11. View of Jackson Street, c. 1900, with the old Union Bank building (*right*), and Larkin House (*center*) opposite Burnham house and shop. Courtesy of Nicholls State University Archives.

Twenty feet wide by fifty feet long, the Larkin building's walls were thirteen inches thick, the second floor accessible by two flights of "common stairs," one outside, one inside. The carpenters were instructed to include four doors, the two front downstairs doors to resemble those of a man named H. Davis. The two upstairs front windows were to have "jib doors," essentially fake doors to allow for the wall decorations to continue across the door surfaces. The house cost $1,540, with Larkin paying for the materials "as we [Springer and Frost] get of Mr. [Sumner] Townsend and deduct from our bill." No interior walls were specified; perhaps Larkin intended the building for commercial use on the first floor, and storage or even residential above, because the second story floorboards were to be "planed on both sides" and "the second joice [*sic*] to be planed." Larkin's instructions to Kees were significant both as evidence of the new association of Maine native Sumner Townsend as a co-owner of the sawmill and as proof that the mill had been upgraded to make it capable of planing boards of lumber on both

IMAGE 12. View of James Frost compound and Presbyterian Church, Thibodaux, c. 1900. Courtesy of Nicholls State University Archives.

sides, not merely creating rough-cut materials. Having that capacity much increased the mill's usefulness to the community.[17]

By the end of the decade, Springer and Frost were no longer working together, and Frost had acquired a large lot for his residence in the center of the town; it was numbered 34 on the Grinage map of 1842 and bounded by the corners of St. Philip and Thibodaux (West Fourth) Streets, St. Louis and St. Bridget (West Fifth) Streets, and St. Philip and St. Bridget Streets. When Frost died in September 1853, the First Presbyterian Church occupied a quarter of the same block, at the corner of St. Louis and Thibodaux. Frost's family took up the rest of the block for a home, outbuildings, orchards, and a stable.

Frost had become a wealthy man; his succession auction inventory contained not only the downtown residence property but two large lots on St. Mary Street, west of Jackson Street, located just above the sawmill and the businesses on the northern end of Jackson's intersection with St. Mary. Numbered 200 and 203 on an 1846 survey by E. D. Richardson, the lots were bounded in front by the public road that skirted Bayou Lafourche, on the east by Church Street, above or west by lot 204, and south by lot 201, property of another resident. Today the site is occupied by Jean Lafitte National Park Acadian Cultural Center, mainly housed in the 1905-era Percy-Lobdell warehouse. In the early 1850s, Frost's land along St. Mary represented an impressively large semi-industrial complex. In addition, in 1850, Springer paid Frost $1,500 for Frost's half-interest in a twenty-foot-wide lot and improvements fronting on Jackson that the partners had acquired from John Larkin in 1847.

In his succession, Frost's residence, his outbuildings, stables, and the home lot occupying three-quarters of the town block were appraised at $3,800 and sold to Frost's widow, Almira. The estate included a number of enslaved men and women. One man named Jake, "a good carpenter," and his wife and two infants also were sold to Almira Frost for $2,200, along with another carpenter named Andie, age thirty, sold for $2,100. Three others, Dan, Aaron, and William, all skilled carpenters, brought $2,000, $2,650, and $1,700 respectively, or a total of $6,350, in a transaction with the Terrebonne planter Van P. Winder. Frost's widow bought from the estate a boy, also named William, age twelve, for $1,200, and the household cook, Harriet, was sold to Almira's mother, Mary B. Ragan, for $875.[18]

The two most highly valued artisans who were bought from the Frost succession by Van P. Winder—Dan and Aaron—were destined soon to

Image 13. Master carpenter James A. Frost, c. 1850. Courtesy of Nicholls State University Archives

participate in another construction adventure. Winder was a brother of Caroline Winder Guion of Ridgefield Plantation and lived at Ducros Plantation along the Terrebonne Road near Terrebonne Station, present-day Schriever. Winder immediately arranged to sell the two enslaved men for what he paid for them, $4,650, to the new partnership of Morgan Springer and Sciotha S. Evans. The two master builders needed the well-trained artisans to help construct a new, grand Ducros Plantation mansion for Van Perkins and Martha Grundy Winder.[19]

CHAPTER SIX

Springer and Evans

A Nest of Builders and Ducros Plantation

Unlike his fellow Pennsylvanian, the master carpenter Morgan Springer waited five years to find a Louisiana bride; she was of French-Acadian stock. Azelie Clementine Bourg and Morgan Springer married in a civil ceremony in the Lafourche Parish courthouse in Thibodaux on January 22, 1846. "Clem," as she was often called, had delivered a daughter the week prior, on January 15, 1846, named Marie Anne Springer. Springer's young wife was born in Thibodaux to Marie Hortense Rosalie Guillot. A native of neighboring Assumption Parish born in 1813, by the age of fifteen Marie Hortense wed Joseph Guillot and gave birth to Clementine on December 19, 1828. The Springer family eventually included seven children.[1] After Morgan's death in August 1861, Azelie Clementine raised the remaining youths on her own, living until July 17, 1918. As of the Census of 1880, then recorded as age fifty, she was "keeping house" and residing with a daughter, Helene, age twenty-eight, and with sons James M., twenty-three, noted as "clerk," and Morgan, age eighteen, an "engineer."[2]

Judging by the 1880 Census, Clementine Springer's home was set in an upscale Thibodaux neighborhood next to a grocer, a lawyer, and a storekeeper.[3] This residence was not the Springers' first. On the same day in 1843 when Frost acquired his lot on the Jackson-St. Mary Street corner, Springer also paid $400 to George S. Guion for a lot on Guion's newly established subdivision on the west side of Jackson Street.[4] Numbered lot 155 on the plan of eleven lots laid out by Guion and certified by James B. Grinage on May 10, 1842, it was 100 feet 3 inches fronting on Jackson by 227 feet 11 inches deep. In the rear, Harrison Street bounded the lot. Next to that lot 155, containing the Springer home and shop, Frost owned the corner lot of Jackson and St. Mary Street until he sold it for the site of Thibodaux's first Methodist church. *The Thibodaux Minerva* later advertised Springer's business location as "Carpenter and Builder, Jackson Street, near the Methodist Church."[5]

While Springer appears to have situated his workshop initially at his home, on March 11, 1847, Frost and Springer paid Dr. Thomas M. Williams for property described officially as three-fourths of an arpent (about 27,600 square feet in area).[6] It was a portion of a large parcel fronting on Jackson Street at or near the corner of St. Mary that Dr. Williams had acquired in 1844. The newly bought L-shaped lot was bounded on the north by the businessmen Arthur M. Foley and Sumner Townsend, who jointly owned the Thibodaux sawmill that had originally belonged to Absalom Kees, and by other land of Kees; on the west by Church Street; and south by St. Mary Street and other property of Dr. Williams. The Springer-Frost property thus fronted on both Jackson and St. Mary, only a short walk from the homes of both builders, Springer on Jackson and now Frost a block away on St. Philip. The newly bought commercial site allowed space for a combined shop operation and perhaps quarters for enslaved workers as well.

The acquisition from Dr. Williams was one of three by Frost and Springer in March 1847. Almost simultaneous with it, and apparently as a means of filling in gaps between the new properties, the builders purchased two other small parcels adjoining the first. One, twenty feet wide fronting on Jackson by seventy-five feet deep, was obtained from the copper, tin, and sheet iron manufacturer John Larkin for $1,800;[7] the other, only twenty feet by twelve feet, was bought for $75 from Charles F. Hawley, the prominent, longtime foundryman who in a few years would depart Thibodaux for Louisville.[8] Within a month of the latter sale in 1847, for $300, Frost and Springer sold to another new carpenter in town, Sciotha S. Evans, a portion of the parcel they had acquired from Dr. Williams. Facing St. Mary in the first block west of Jackson Street, the lot was 132 feet in depth on the east (Jackson Street/Dr. Williams) side and eighty-six feet wide on the north backing up to the saw-mill property. Evans, a Missouri native destined to become Springer's partner when Frost went on his own a few years later, soon constructed his home and shop on the deep lot.[9] The Frost-Springer partnership progressed through the late 1840s, and, like Kees, Springer often gained election to the city council, serving in 1849–1850, 1854, and 1857.[10] Springer's knowledge of construction was politically useful. In 1848, for example, the mayor named him to a committee "to superintend the paving [sidewalks] of the town," and the partners sold to the town the bricks for paving.[11] They were well positioned to benefit from public construction contracts. One such arrangement in June 1847 was for an office on the courthouse lot for the Lafourche Parish clerk of court and designed "similar to the Recorder's Office." Described in the recorded building contract, the brick structure was raised off the ground eighteen inches and built twenty-four feet wide by thirty-five feet deep. It was to contain two rooms, each with a fireplace and mantel, each room's ceiling to be twelve feet high, and the walls were to be plastered and painted. The building's west front was adorned with "a twelve foot gallery" and "six large windows with shutters in front room and commodious front door, covered with sheet iron." Besides featuring a back door, the rear room contained windows with "roling [*sic*] blinds." The roof of the structure was described "of good sound slate." In addition to what the specifications required, Frost and Springer agreed to construct either a picket or a "planke" fence around the house lot. For their work, the parish contracted to pay the builders $1,400.[12]

Probably before 1850, Frost established his own business on the newly acquired lots 200 and 203 a short distance up St. Mary Street. In December 1850 he sold to Springer his half-interest in the property they jointly bought in 1847 fronting on St. Mary.[13] Soon after his death in 1853, Frost's lots containing his shop were valued in his succession at $2,200. Only the home lot on the corner of St. Philip and St. Bridget in the center of town was appraised higher, at $3,800. Frost died a successful, prosperous businessman with wide, helpful connections in the community of Thibodaux. His estate, including ten people held in servitude, came to a total worth of $20,195, equal to about $755,000 in 2024 dollars.[14]

When Springer's new partner, Sciotha S. Evans, arrived in Thibodaux midway in the antebellum years, the town was booming. Her population had more than doubled between 1840 and 1850, and the number of carpenters had grown to at least twenty-five. A native of Missouri born about 1823, Sciotha S. Evans (also known as "S. S. Evans") left home sometime in the late 1840s, but his apparent arrival in Lafourche Parish is not reflected in the United States Census of 1850.[15] By 1860 and living at dwelling 10, Evans was occupied as a carpenter and married to wife Mary Jane.[16] The couple had four daughters. Evans owned and kept at home an enslaved woman (aged twenty-four at the time of the census).[17] He additionally co-owned with Morgan Springer a thirty-year-old enslaved man. In the late 1880s, by then widowered and after a long career as one of Thibodaux's premier builders, Evans left the Lafourche region and returned to his birthplace, in Center, Call County, Missouri. An obituary in *The Weekly Thibodaux Sentinel* by

Silas Grisamore described Evans as "an old and respected citizen who resided in this town during 50 years."[18]

Grisamore may have been slightly off his count; there is no record of Evans in Thibodaux prior to 1847, when he bought from Springer and Frost the lot facing St. Mary Street near its corner with Jackson Street.[19] He departed Louisiana in 1886, after he sold the lot to John McCulla for $900.[20] We can be assured, too, that soon following his 1847 purchase Evans was in Thibodaux building his shop and residence. Dating his efforts is an 1848 courthouse record showing Evans indebted to a carpenter/mason, Henry Fleming, for $297 on promissory notes for "work done by . . . Fleming to a house" on "the western side of Jackson street."[21] The lot contained the same dimensions as those in the sale by Springer and Frost to Evans. The home that Evans built in 1848 soon contained a wife, Mary Jane Elam, a seventeen-year-old native of Kentucky who at the time of the marriage on November 13, 1850, lived at Bayou Sara in West Feliciana Parish.[22] By the time of the census count in 1860, the family had added four girls.[23]

IMAGE 14. Ducros Plantation House, Terrebonne Parish, c. 1880. Courtesy of Nicholls State University Archives.

With James Frost entering into a sole proprietorship and moving his carpentry affairs up St. Mary Street, Springer and Evans joined forces. They soon undertook a grand enterprise that kept them occupied at least until Springer's death and Evans alone thereafter: the construction of the Ducros Plantation house. Facing Bayou Terrebonne and still a grand Greek Revival-style house with a notable history, Ducros stands just north of what was known as Terrebonne Station, now named Schriever, and three miles south of Thibodaux.

Among the Anglo-American entrepreneurs who settled along Bayous Black and Terrebonne in the 1830s were Van Perkins (or Van P.) Winder of Natchez and his wife Martha Grundy Winder. Martha was a daughter of President Andrew Jackson's legislative ally from Tennessee, United States Senator Felix Grundy, who became the US attorney general under President Martin Van Buren. Van Winder shared a half-interest in a Terrebonne Parish plantation on Bayou Black with his sister Caroline Winder Guion of Ridgefield Plantation. In 1841, Winder sold the Bayou Black interest and acquired a share in Southdown Plantation from James Dinsmore for $31,000. The Southdown Plantation transaction made him a partner of the Natchez native and landowner John Minor, who had employed Absalom Kees in the 1820s. Following a buyout by Minor in 1845, the Winders acquired 1,200 acres of Ducros Plantation. Their admiration of and connections with Andrew Jackson may have persuaded them to model their new home after Jackson's famous residence near Nashville, the Hermitage. The Winders' undertaking required well-trained artisans.[24]

Van Winder learned about James Frost's death in 1853 and, surely through advertisement of the inventoried succession, of Frost's five highly valued enslaved carpenters. On January 7, 1854, when the succession sale occurred, Winder bought three of Frost's enslaved artisans. He promptly sold two of them to "Morgan Springer and Susto [*sic*] S. Evans." One, described as "Dan, a Negro Man a good carpenter, aged thirty-five years," sold for $2,000, and "Aaron, a Negro boy, a good carpenter, aged thirty years," sold for $2,650.[25] These purchases, followed by quick resales, were no coincidence: Winder immediately hired the master carpenters, Springer and Evans, to begin work on his Ducros Plantation house. Although the identity of the architect for Ducros is unknown, the two carpenters exerted a great influence on the character of the house. It remains in use today as a rental for

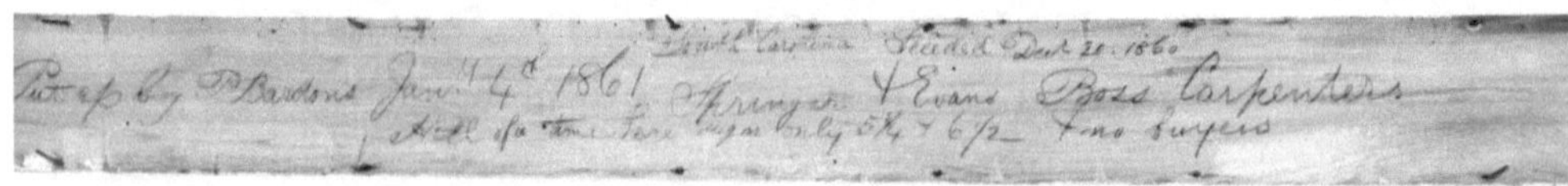

IMAGE 15. Carpenter Inscription at Ducros Plantation House.
Courtesy of Richard Bourgeois.

weddings and other functions, after the current owner, Richard Bourgeois of Houma, spent many years undertaking its restoration.

Building Ducros extended beyond the start of the Civil War. After Van Winder died of yellow fever in 1854, his widow Martha Grundy Winder continued to oversee the work. When the Civil War commenced, Springer and Evans were still laboring to complete the home. Writing on a door frame in January 1861, a worker marked, “South Carolina seceded Dec 20 1860 Put up by P Bardons Jany 4 1861 Springer & Evans Boss Carpenters Hell of a time here sugar only 5¾ & 6½ & no buyers.”[26]

Morgan Springer died in the summer of 1861; his succession inventory, completed September 9, 1861, included the half-interest in the enslaved men bought from Van P. Winder, who “belong to the firm of Springer & Evans jointly.” Aaron and Dan, each “a carpenter by trade,” were valued at $1,250 and $1,125, respectively.[27] The succession revealed, too, that although Martha Winder had compensated the partners for some of the work at the Ducros Plantation using a promissory note for $14,132.18, she still owed the money to the firm of Springer and Evans. The sizable debt by Martha Winder to Springer and Evans may have represented sums for other construction besides that on her residence. Details are not spelled out, and because a construction plan and contract have not been located, there is no evidence that Ducros House was completed. According to Richard Bourgeois, the Winder family remained economically stressed and was forced to sell their property not long after the Civil War.[28] The debt to Evans and the succession of Springer alone represents a value of more than $504,000 in 2024 dollars.

CHAPTER SEVEN

Bellsen, Springer, and Evans

Two Notable Parish Jails and a Courthouse for the Age

By 1850, Thibodaux had become a major regional center of trade, industry, and government. Its population numbered around one thousand. Noted in statistics of the 1850 Census, many of the town's citizens originated from other states, and more than 162 people were of foreign origin, notably those native to France and Ireland; a smattering came from Germany, England, and other countries. The people of Thibodaux and her close proximity occupied a variety of callings, in which the construction trades dominated: at least twenty-five heads of households termed themselves builders or carpenters, and the town hosted five masons or bricklayers and four painters or plasterers.[1]

During the prior decade, the community added two major town-sponsored landmarks: a marketplace was built in the town square across Market Street (currently West Second) from the old wooden courthouse, and Guion Academy public school was erected on Jackson at the corner of Clinton (today West Tenth) Street. The town progressed in brick paving for the sidewalks, called banquettes (street paving would await another age), and in draining rain runoff. After suffering since its founding from almost nonexistent waste disposal and control over wandering animals, the town had banned large animal meanderings and established a location for and a system of disposing of household and market refuse. The dumping of animal carcasses in the bayou and in the canal connecting it with Bayou Terrebonne, however, remained a problem. All houses had outdoor toilets, and the council enacted ordinances requiring side- or backyard privies to be located away from sidewalks. Backyards, where animals were kept, required fencing.[2]

From only a few brick structures in 1840, the 1850 town struck the visitor with the sight of many handsome brick residences and commercial and governmental buildings. The rosy outlook continued into the 1850s, as

The Thibodaux Minerva's optimistic comments on August 6, 1853, illustrate: "Buildings we are pleased to say, continue to rise in different parts," and "the noise of the trowel, hammer and saw, greet our ears, no matter whither we may wander."[3] At least three large Protestant churches and the (soon replaced) St. Joseph's Catholic Church just east of the town limits provided places of worship.

However, in the number and quality of major governmental structures, the town lagged. From the time of its construction, the parish courthouse was often used for public meetings and church worship. It now was badly outdated and neglected. The jail, placed across Main Street from the courthouse, was disgraceful, unhealthy, and decrepit. It could be described as coming from another, more primitive era. The entire decade of the 1850s passed before remedies were completed at the jail and on the courthouse square.

Two master carpenter firms would have large roles to play. In 1859, the partnership of Morgan Springer and Sciotha Evans remained busy at the Winder home, the Ducros Plantation house. One might think that undertaking a large construction job for Martha Grundy Winder a few miles south of town would allow for little else. Over the 1850s, however, the contractors continued with various other projects. And, as noted earlier, they served at times as trustees on the city council. Their list of work included homes or business establishments for prominent citizens of the town. As an illustration, in the winter of 1857–1858 they completed a "Brick House built by us as per contract," for which the men received $2,000 from "Mrs. Heloise Knoblock job of Mr. T. Bernard."[4] Their close contacts with the municipal government also brought them business; as an example, they received $125 on February 21, 1855, for unspecified work and another sum for repairs at the Guion Academy, on May 8, 1858. The firm bid $2,700 for a lucrative job to construct a wharf on the edge of Bayou Lafourche in front of the town's business section. It lost out to Michel Dué, who received the work when he bid $2,500.[5]

The challenges of the Lafourche Parish jail and courthouse opened greater opportunities for major public projects. Lafourche Parish Record D, the earliest preserved record of Lafourche Parish police jury meetings, begins in 1852. For a depiction of the courthouse and jailhouse squares before then, we rely upon personal observations, and few remain. Silas Grisamore wrote in 1890 in his *Weekly Thibodaux Sentinel* that the early courthouse was a wood-frame structure. As noted, it provided a place not only for local government functions but for various civic exhibitions, meetings, dances, and other recreational gatherings. Members of various church denominations "held prayers" and services at the old structure as well. In the northeast corner of the courthouse square there "was a small building used for the office of the district clerk of court, and the northwest corner of the square held a similar building, occupied by the recorder of the parish."[6] The original jail, like the courthouse of wood-frame construction, sat on the same site as the structure known today as the old jail, remodeled in the art deco mode in the 1930s; it presently is a part of the Lafourche Parish clerk of court complex situated at the south corner of the intersection of Green and Main Streets, across Main Street from the courthouse.[7]

Despite the run-down conditions of both jail and courthouse, the police jury waited until well past 1850 to consider any changes. Reflecting the police jurors' initial concerns during the September 1852 session, the jury recorder stated, "It is of the utmost importance that some steps should be taken . . . relative to the construction of a new Court House suited to the convenience of the Parish." Once selected, a building committee's members were charged to "cause some plans & specifications to be made for . . . a neat and commodious Court House not to exceed Fifteen Thousand Dollars and to make their report at the next session." No progress was made; the following March 1853, the committee had in hand "a plan and specifications," not for a courthouse, but for a jail. There was no explanation for the change in direction, but the "several [jail] propositions" that the police jury received ensured a delay until July 1853. Then, the jury determined to reject "the proposition of Mr. Bellson [Assumption resident who ultimately built a new Lafourche Parish jail] for building" a jail. No reason was given for turning down Bellsen's offer.[8]

Probably because of the devastations in Thibodaux caused by the yellow fever epidemic of 1853 between late July and November, the courthouse square project stalled. And matters at the jail worsened: in 1854 the jail committee found the "privy of said yard . . . in an horrible dirty condition." It seems to have served as a public outhouse, because the jury noted that after the sheriff had it "put in order," the privy should be locked up "except during the session of the District Court and Police Jury." The jailor, who had the use and care of the grounds, received the caution to "remove the weeds from the yard and keep the inclosure [*sic*] in good orders." Perhaps to assist him in weed maintenance, the jailor obtained permission to "keep a calf and a horse" there, but he must "run all risks and damages that might occur."[9] By June 1855 one J. D. Besson became the jailor, but another year passed before the police jury decided what to do about the parish's disgraceful house of incarceration. During the jury's June 1856 session, its members determined not to attempt repair but to build a new jail. They again "authorized a plan made to build a new jail . . . and to find out on what conditions and for what price said jail could be built in brick according to said plan." Three prominent citizens, Sumner Townsend,[10] John C. Beatty (or Beattie), and V. Vicknair, were designated "to carry forward" and to repair the fence enclosing the courthouse and jail or to build a new enclosure if needed.[11]

The presence of Townsend and Beatty on the police jury committee is significant. Both at times belonged to St. John's Episcopal Church. Townsend served on the building committee of St. John's, which in June 1856 contracted to renovate the church structure. Its renovation architect was the noteworthy Irish native Henry Howard, then living and practicing in New Orleans.[12] The likelihood is that during the same year, perhaps in June, Howard became the architect for the new Lafourche Parish jail. The Townsend and Beatty connections with the famed New Orleans architect, whose lifetime creations numbered in the hundreds, must have helped determine his choice as the architect for the new jail and later for a new courthouse.

The evidence of Howard's hire in 1856 to design a new jail is missing. None of the police jury minutes mentions Howard that year, and the jury may have obtained estimates from another source; but at its September session, the group resolved to set an ad valorem tax of fifteen cents on each one hundred dollars of value "for the purpose of paying the current expenses of the parish jurors for their services and to erect a suitable and substantial jail in the parish." To establish a tax, the jury evidently had received good estimates from Howard of the cost for the jail.[13]

More delays took place until August 1857, when the police jury again appointed a committee to adopt "a plan and specifications for the jail, choosing a location, and contracting with power to bind the Parish, for the construction of the jail."[14] The police jury proposed to pay the contractor a first cash installment from a so-called "surplus fund" and to finance the balance of the cost through an ad valorem tax on property subject to such taxation. By then, the old jail had attracted continued attention from the grand jury.

Its findings spelled out to the district court the "unhealthy," "pestilential," "filthy and nauseating" conditions, "a state of dilapidation and insecurity," and an absence of "bedding bags and other requisites what little now is furnished them being supplied by the jailor himself."[15]

The district court's threats of criminal prosecution, combined with political shame, apparently moved matters to a conclusion. The police jury hired its architect, Henry Howard, and his partner, Albert Diettel, to draw plans. In May 1858 the jury signed the building contract with the original 1853 bidder, John Bellsen, who then was nearing completion of the newly formed St. Matthew's Episcopal Church in Houma.[16] Given Howard's already-strong presence in the Lafourche region, his choice to design St. Matthew's was no coincidence. The police jury's authority to contract with Bellsen for a new jail is stated in the preamble to the terms, referring to the "ordinance relative to the building of a public jail and the raising of the necessary funds passed the 27th day of August 1857."[17] During the summer of 1858, the jury set a jail construction budget of $9,000, but at the completion in June 1859, the police jury minutes noted a cost "recapitulation" with a refigured total cost of $15, 391.56.[18] The arrangement with Bellsen in 1858 had specified a total price of $10,265, including all materials; the building committee foresaw that alterations to the plans would occur and made provision for them. As an example, the agreement noted that Bellsen should use "English iron," rather than iron made in the United States, "for the iron grating required to go round the center of the exterior."[19] For a complicated edifice like a "modern" jail, a precise cost was difficult to pin down. Still, the large amount over budget must have been a hard pill for local politicians to swallow.

Like many of the Thibodaux area building contracts of the time, the 1858 Lafourche parish jail architectural drawings drafted by Howard and guiding Bellsen are lost. The contract between the parties is sparse on details and refers to Howard's specifications only in the briefest of terms: "marked (A) and the three plans marked (B), (C) & (D)."[20] Some nineteenth-century jail photos remain. They depict a square, fortress-like structure of two stories "topped with a belvedere with two full Roman arched windows on each of its four sides." Its walls featured a "crenellated parapet above a denticulated cornice."[21] In March 1860, the police jury began a process of auctioning off the lumber, bricks, and iron remaining from the demolition of the original jailhouse. With the onset of the Civil War a year later, the jail received a new function, when the police jury authorized "the Military Board" to use the structure for "depositing arms and ammunition, and . . . to have such changes or alterations made as may be necessary for the purpose, without . . . deranging any of the walls."[22]

John Bellsen's importance in any story of builders in and around antebellum Thibodaux cannot be neglected. Born in 1814 in New York to German or Dutch parents, by the 1840s Bellsen was residing in Assumption Parish. The parish records show him owning land and enslaved persons. His farming operation was not major: the *Statement of the Sugar Crop Made in Louisiana, 1845–1846* by P. A. Champomier notes Bellsen's production from the year's crop at only twenty-two hogsheads, among the least in the parish.[23] Following an active 1850s as a builder in Assumption, Lafourche, and Terrebonne Parishes, Bellsen moved to Marksville in Avoyelles Parish, where by 1860 he was a "keeper of [a] Lumber Yard," his real estate valued at $30,000. In September 1861, Bellsen married Sarah Elizabeth Barbre in Pointe Coupee Parish. She was born in Kentucky in 1832 and at the time of marriage also resided in Avoyelles Parish.[24]

A natural question to ask is how John Bellsen became qualified to construct a special-purpose structure like the Lafourche Parish jail, requiring hard-to-obtain materials and highly technical competence. The record of Bellsen's experience before he arrived in Louisiana is virtually missing, but the Assumption Parish police jury found in John Belsen the qualifications needed for building its own new jail in 1853, five years before Lafourche commenced a new house of incarceration.

A contract between the Assumption Parish government and John Bellsen was signed in the parish seat of Napoleonville, Louisiana, on December 13, 1853.[25] It required Bellsen to build a new prison where "the old jail now stands," next to and upstream from the Assumption courthouse. Thirty feet wide and forty-three feet long "from out to out of main walls," the two-story structure was raised three feet off the ground. The first story was eleven feet high, the upper story ten feet. Bellsen agreed to use "best hard and well burnt country made bricks laid in mortar of fresh Thomaston lime and clean sharp sand." The walls contained four windows, each six feet eight inches high, forty-two inches wide, all openings to be shuttered by "two fold moulded and bead and butt panel shutters well hung with all necessary bolts and latches of the best quality." The jail budget was $4,482, of which $1,500 was paid to Bellsen when the contract was signed, $1,491 scheduled upon delivery on September 1, 1854, and the balance, $1,491, due twelve months

IMAGE 16. Lafourche Parish jail, c. 1895.
Courtesy of Nicholls State University Archives.

after the completion of the work. No architect is named in the Assumption jail contract, but in all likelihood, Henry Howard played a part. He had designed and supervised the building of two of the major antebellum Greek Revival-style homes in Louisiana, Woodlawn (1845–1849) and Madewood (1846–1849), both mansions situated just below Napoleonville on the left bank of Bayou Lafourche.[26] Significantly, among those in the parish committee signing the jail contract was William W. Pugh, owner of Woodlawn.

Turning again to Lafourche Parish, despite the difficulties in providing a new jail in 1858, the parish leaders were not done with their major improvements. Simultaneous with Bellsen's completion of the Lafourche jail, the police jury finally determined upon a new courthouse and selected its architect, the firm of Howard & Diettel: a natural choice, given those architects' close connections with Thibodaux and their work on the new jail. However, awarding the firm a courthouse design contract would have to wait: first, the parish must determine its location. Police Jury Resolution No. 22 of June 6, 1859, described the parish's intention "to build a new, convenient and suitable Court House . . . on the same lot on which the public jail has been built to serve as a Court room, Jury room, Clerk's office, Recorder's office and Sheriff's office."[27]

Anticipating a quick start, the parish authorized a cost of $20,000, of which one-fourth would be paid to the builders in cash down, and the rest spread over three payments in March 1860, 1861, and 1862. It also formed a committee of Patrick H. Gary, Cleophas Lagarde, John Lyell, C. F. Gaudé, and O. L. Blanchard to prepare the plans and specifications, to sign a building contract for the erection "of such Court house and inclosures [*sic*]," and "to employ at a reasonable salary a competent person to superintend the erection." By late June 1859, the police jury had its plans and specifications from architects Howard & Diettel; the firm received $500 for the design work. But, soon following the receipt of the plans, the police jury made an about-face on the courthouse location. Perhaps the parish leaders considered a physical arrangement that abutted it with the jail diminished the courthouse's public appearance and attractiveness. Giving the new courthouse more prominence by facing it to the central market square and Bayou Lafourche also made good political and aesthetic sense. In their July 18, 1859, session, the jurors passed Resolution No. 27 allowing (but not requiring) the courthouse committee to change the site "to the lot where now is situated the courthouse, and as near the center of said lot as practicable."[28] It left the final decision to the committee, which also obtained the authority to pay for the erection of the structure as the work progressed, rather than paying part down and part thereafter in regular installments. The parish advertised for the builder in newspapers, among them the *Daily Picayune* of New Orleans. By mid-September 1859, the police jury awarded the work to the master carpenter firm of Morgan Springer and Sciotha S. Evans. The contractors did not sign the agreement to build and work specifications until November 13. Having demonstrated such high-quality work in the community, the two men may have been an "only choice."[29] They also enjoyed helpful political contacts: Springer served as a trustee on the town council in 1857, and Evans became a trustee in 1858, reelected in 1859.[30]

Surely site preparations for the new building were underway even before the master builders signed the work agreement that autumn of 1859. By December, however, the police jury continued to tussle with the existing parish courthouse and its removal. It empowered the building committee to sell the old structure to the highest bidder, remove it from the square, and "rent a room in the town . . . for the holding of Sessions of the Court until the new Court House be finished." If unsold, the old building should be moved onto the jail lot, to be "placed on opposite corner of the gail [*sic*], and on a line therewith the back of the present jailor's house." Court sessions might then continue in the old structure. Thereafter it "could be repaired and arranged to serve for a jailor's house." Last, the two other houses located on the courthouse square "used as offices by the Recorder and Clerk" might be sold.[31] The parish government was much challenged with overlapping and ongoing work in the public squares occupied by the courthouse and the jail.

As things progressed in 1860, the police jury struggled with both the construction cost and the ad valorem taxes needed to pay for the new courthouse. Various and sometimes conflicting or confusing accounts are recorded in the Minute Book D. For example, on June 4, 1860, the record shows a "balance on hand" amount of $6,656 out of a total for that year so far of $10,025.14, as well as another $3,339.21½. At a later 1860 session, the parish paid an additional $5,000 out of its current budget of $13,000; and in June 1861, in a recapitulation, it paid $8,000 for the courthouse work, followed by $4,650. In December 1860, confronted with Louisiana's secession from the United States and a war increasingly likely, Lafourche Parish faced a dilemma. It needed funds to pay for a memorial for a military organization known as the "Creole Guards" but backed off any contribution: "the present liabilities of the Parish resulting from the construction of the Court House, and the Contingent expenses of the parish, will exceed the assets perhaps by some $3,000," those moneys to be provided by loans, paid for out of assets to be collected.[32] After Morgan Springer died in August 1861, his succession showed that the two carpenters were owed $4,770.[33] It is unclear whether Springer's heirs and Evans ever received the amount due them from Lafourche Parish.

Springer and Evans undertook the courthouse construction while they were still responsible to Martha Winder at her Ducros home near Terrebonne Station. They may have considered the Lafourche Parish government a more stable source of employ. The parish could rely on tax funding, whereas the work at Ducros appears to have been a fits-and-starts situation, its progress funded mainly when the plantation sugarcane crops thrived and sugar prices were good. Even with their own crews of enslaved artisans and hirelings,

Springer and Evans faced real challenges to bring workers and suppliers simultaneously to the courthouse and the Ducros jobs.

Some on-site assistance may have been provided by the firm of Howard & Diettel, which probably rented a temporary office in Thibodaux on St. Philip Street. The architects had other jobs ongoing in the country parishes, but their main sources of employ were in New Orleans. There, multiple residences and commercial buildings and at least one church were underway between 1859 and 1861. In the midst of that time, too, Diettel left Howard to form a new partnership with a fellow German native, William Thiel. In May 1860, Howard associated with another architect, Henry Thiberge. Then a youth of twenty-three, Thiberge remained with Howard only until 1861, but the two architects reunited in partnership around 1880 or 1881. In the interim, in 1875 Thiberge had been incarcerated in the Lafourche Parish jail on a charge of murdering a suspect that he was deputized to arrest near Raceland for

raping a child in New Orleans. While in jail awaiting trial, Thiberge was contacted by Dr. Hercules Dansereau of Thibodaux, who persuaded the imprisoned New Orleans architect to design the renovation of his raised cottage on St. Philip Street, near the business district. Originally the home of Dr. James A. Scudday, an early mayor, the structure faced the street on a large lot. Remodeled in the mansard roof style of Napoleon III, the impressive old mansion remains known today as the Dansereau House. In June 1876, Thiberge, convicted in a Lafourche Parish jury trial and sentenced to hang, received support from the community, including the sentencing judge, Taylor Beattie. Prominent locals petitioned Governor William R. Kellogg to commute the architect's sentence.[34]

After receiving a full pardon and his freedom, Thiberge resided and worked in Thibodaux for a while before he returned to his architecture business in New Orleans, where he reunited with Howard for the rest of

IMAGE 17. "Thibodeauville Bayou Lafourche," Alfred E. Waud etching of downtown Thibodaux, 1871. Courtesy of the Historic New Orleans Collection, accession 1966.21.

Howard's life. Thiberge, too, had a hand in work on the courthouse and jail: in 1879, the parish contracted with him for repair work on both structures and for a new iron picket fence around the courthouse. Dr. Hercules Dansereau, his close friend and apparent savior, became Thiberge's bonded security for completion of the work.[35]

What we do not know about the construction of the Lafourche Parish courthouse from 1859 to 1861 is tantalizing. What was a typical daily work routine on the courthouse square? How many people were at the jobsite on an average day? How much were the various workers paid and how frequently? Who oversaw their tasks and the pace of work? What men in bondage were forced to work there, and where were they from? As the Civil War approached and began, did the work experience slowdowns or interruptions?

Thankfully, the agreement to build the courthouse, containing the contract specifications, survived. The documents now are part of a group of almost 28,000 old records allowed by the Lafourche Parish district court judges and former clerk of court, Vernon Rodrigue, to be housed at the Nicholls State University Archives. Over ten years, a number of volunteers of Lafourche Heritage Society—especially Goldie Legendre and Marjorie Landry, directed by university archivists Carol Mathias and Clifton Theriot—carefully cataloged the documents. The archivists and volunteers formed a large database for a collection of mainly nineteenth-century parish government records that give researchers a rare view into the life of Lafourche Parish and its government in the antebellum and postbellum eras.[36]

The courthouse building contract is known as "Specifications of a Building for a Parish Court House to be erected in the town of Thibodaux, La." Dated September 15, 1859, and signed on November 13, 1859, it was the agreement between the builders, Springer and Evans, and the building committee members, J. F. Thompson, Patrick. H. Gary, O. L. Blanchard, Charles. F. Gaudet, and C. Lagarde. Of them, at least Patrick Gary, owner of a foundry, had served with Springer as a town trustee earlier in the 1850s. The men all were influential in the town's business community. Gary and Thompson, for example, were officials of the important Thibodaux Bridge Company, which in the late 1850s completed the first bridge across Bayou Lafourche at Jackson Street.[37]

In preparation for their task, the contractors needed to assemble a large variety of artisans and suppliers. The specifications listed bricklayers, stonemasons, blacksmiths, founders, coppersmiths, slaters, carpenters and joiners, plasterers, painters, and glaziers. In order to complete their tasks, they required materials from businesses such as sawmills, foundries, brick makers and brick yards, Welsh slate mines, stone quarries, iron mines, and various mills in the eastern United States. No less crucial, shipping those materials to the site required sailing vessels, Mississippi River flatboats and steamboats, and the New Orleans, Opelousas and Great Western Railroad. Of great service, the railroad then extended from the west bank of the river across from downtown New Orleans to a station at Lafourche Crossing (four miles to the east of town) on to Terrebonne Station (four miles south) and beyond to Brashear's Landing on the Atchafalaya River. The courthouse work received supervision not just from Springer and Evans but others whose experience and acumen allowed them to oversee the special tasks underway. While the foundations were laid and the erection and finishing were ongoing, local businesses supplied food and beverages. The master carpenters had a number of their own enslaved artisans, and workers from local plantations or independent businesses could be rented to the contractors for the heavy labor.

Considering the high number, variety, and skill level of workers in demand to assist in the creation of the courthouse, their availability is a question. Probably some specialists and common laborers came from New Orleans, arriving by train at Lafourche Crossing late on the weekends and returning to the city at the end of work weeks. In addition, according to the Census of 1860, the town of Thibodaux and her close environs could supply a large number of artisans. An exact count of them is difficult, but as an example of craftsmen in the building trades in Thibodaux (Ward 7b), the census shows four brick masons; on the outskirts (Ward 7), another five masons, two master masons, and two apprentice masons are identified. The town counted six painters, a finisher, and two plasterers; two more painters resided on the outskirts.[38]

The attention to full detail in the building contract is striking, spelling out what materials to use, what must be done, and how the work should be carried out. (See Appendix A for a reproduction of the contract.) Some samples of the specifications help make the point here:

Under "Bricklayers' Work," with regard to "Slates and Cement": "There shall be two courses of the brickwork laid in fresh hydraulic cement mortar and a course of strong new Welch slates laid in the cement above them, round all the walls and brickwork at the height of 12 inches above the upper offsets to prevent the ascent of moisture."

IMAGE 18. The (Howard-designed) Lafourche Parish courthouse front, c. 1865, photographed by Gustavus Fagersteen. Courtesy of Nicholls State University Archives.

IMAGE 19. Lafourche Parish courthouse and jail, c. 1897.
Courtesy of Nicholls State University Archives.

IMAGE 20. The remodeled (Favrot and Livaudais) Lafourche Parish courthouse, c. 1915. Courtesy of Nicholls State University Archives.

Under "Blacksmith and Founders' Work," with regard to "Iron Work for Vaults": "The doorway of each vault shall have a pair of doors on the inside, and a single door on the outside; the inside doors to be made of No. 10 sheet iron riveted on 1½ x ½ inch wrought iron frame work, and well hung to 2½ x ½ inch wrought iron frames, and secured with strong iron bolts and padlock."

Under "Carpenters' and Joiners' Work," with regard to "Timbers and Plank": "All the timbers and plank used in the erection of the building shall be of the best description of the sound Yellow Pine or Cypress, proper for the uses for which it is designed, free from unsound knots, splits or rot."[39]

Little remained unattended in the specifications: materials must be the most modern and superior, no matter where obtained; workmanship must be thorough, set to the highest standards; and accomplishing the work must be a joint, complete effort. The specifications, like the "accompanying plans, elevations, and sections designed and prepared by Howard and Diettel architects," had been drafted by Howard and his firm.[40] And the original copy of the contract to build is in Henry Howard's clear handwriting.

A picture of the new Lafourche Parish courthouse was taken a few years after its completion by a photographer named Gustavus Fagersteen, who was a German native then working out of a studio in New Orleans before he removed to California. Considering the time and place, the courthouse was a remarkably designed structure. Howard's biographers Brantley and McGee termed the edifice "neo-Roman" in design. It prominently showed both Greek Revival (e.g., fluted Doric columns) and Roman (e.g., full arched windows) elements. The building's entrance portico was enclosed by four tall columns, all facing Market (now Second) Street. Across the intervening market square, the commercially busy Bayou Lafourche flowed. The Fagersteen photo depicts the building surrounded by a white, wooden picket fence. To the left rear one sees the new jail, a dark, small fortress. To the far right of the structure, in the distance, the Presbyterian Church bell tower is seen. The parish later added a Greek Revival-style portico entrance to the courthouse's west side, which faced Green Street rather than Bayou Lafourche. The altered building, pictured c. 1915, featured a Beaux Arts style overall, using a design by the nationally recognized firm of Favrot and Livaudais of New Orleans.[41] The present appearance (not illustrated) of the courthouse retains the c. 1915 style, but the original 1859–1860 portico regrettably was removed to add on parish offices to the original front.

Morgan Springer died in August 1861, shortly after the completion of the Lafourche Parish courthouse, and any record of additional work by Sciotha S. Evans during the Civil War has not been located. Evans survived the conflict and further contributed his talents to the community. The combined efforts of the master carpenters Springer and Evans in the antebellum time had been immense, and some of their creations remain to the present in Thibodaux and environs.

CHAPTER EIGHT

Burnham

A Connecticut Yankee in Thibodaux

In an old book of Lafourche Parish marriage records, a notation dated April 1, 1839, informs us that Edward T. Burnham and Louise Delphine Braud married. He is identified as a "son of the late Eleazor Burnham and Sarah Norton, born in Hartford Connecticut." Also called Lucy or Lucie, Louise Delphine was born to Honoré Braud and Marie Felicité Trahan. Vincent Maggioli, perhaps a Braud relative, served "as security for Burnham in his obtaining a license" to marry; the couple evidently used a local official to perform a civil ceremony.[1]

As this work has shown, the presence of New Englanders in antebellum Bayou Lafourche was not unusual, but a few more examples will help. Soon after Thibodaux's founding, the Rhode Island native Andrew Collins moved to the Lafourche, where he established China Grove Plantation just below Thibodaux on the left descending bank of the bayou. Like Collins, a founder of St. John's Episcopal Church, Charles F. Hawley arrived in Thibodaux from Vermont and became a major foundryman in the town in the 1830s.[2] He was soon followed by Shubael Tenney of eastern Massachusetts, who began the Thibodaux Female Institute, one of the first Protestant schools in the town.[3] The village of Thibodaux attracted migrants from around the entire United States.

Edward Truman Burnham, a master carpenter, at first appears to have settled in Assumption Parish, but he soon found his way to Thibodaux. There, with the help of a credit sale, in February 1837 Burnham acquired from grocer Joseph R. Niles a handsomely situated property. It was forty feet wide fronting on Jackson Street, with a depth of 140 feet. Located on the corner of Jackson and St. Bridget (West Fifth) Streets, the land at the time of this writing is occupied by the Thibodaux branch of the Lafourche Parish library. The Burnham homesite sat across St. Bridget from the soon-to-be-built Union Bank of Louisiana branch and backed up to lots facing St. Philip Street and owned by Madame Brigitte Belanger Thibodaux but shortly to become the home site of Dr. James A. Scudday.[4] In the Burnham house complex, his shop faced St. Bridget Street. Eventually, the Burnhams' neighbors included the home and business of an undertaker named Jake Weber (or Jacob Webre).[5]

Burnham found himself among a large number of other construction artisans, among them Kees, then Springer and Frost, and later Evans. They shared business contacts and learned from each other. When it was built across Jackson Street in the 1840s, Burnham attended the First Methodist Church, along with Kees and Frost. Although Burnham acquired the property at Jackson and St. Bridget as his own in March 1837, the next month he associated a partner, Appolos Randel, who agreed to share profits and expenses.[6] Those included the debts represented by the promissory notes with which Burnham had bought his property. The association was short-lived: Randel soon defaulted on his half of the debts, causing Burnham problems with creditors.[7] The two men annulled their partnership in April 1844, and Randel reimbursed Burnham for the two promissory notes already paid and forsook any interest in the property.[8] By then able to pay off the remaining debt, Burnham resumed the sole ownership of his property.

During his early years in Thibodaux, Burnham appears not to have recorded written contracts for work. He did require help in his trade and, even before acquiring the property on Jackson, recorded an apprenticeship transaction in January 1837. Under the agreement, Burnham took in Joseph Marcellus Molaison, an eighteen-year-old son of Joseph Molaison, "to learn the art, trade, mystery or occupation of carpenter and house joiner which said Burnham now uses, and to dwell and continue with the said Burnham" until young Joseph reached age twenty-one. Apprentice arrangements were unusual for Thibodaux. The New Englander Burnham at first may have been uncomfortable with lifelong enslaved labor, preferring temporary labor to help fill his needs. He agreed to teach the youth his trade and to provide "suitable board and lodgings and meat & drink, washing, mending, & medicine in sickness and health." Instead of giving him clothing, Burnham paid his apprentice $75 the first year, $100 the second year, and $125 the last year. In addition, Burnham committed to "instruct [Molaison] in reading, writing, and arithemetic [*sic*]" to the extent to which Burnham was able.[9] Once again, in 1843, Burnham made arrangements to apprentice another youth, age sixteen, named Louis Edward Lamoureaux. In this instance, the pay for clothing started at only $50, increasing by $10 a year for the four years of apprenticeship. The contract contained no teaching arrangements, and, perhaps having learned a lesson with Molaison, Burnham explicitly relieved himself of responsibility "for offenses or quasi offenses or other acts of Lamoureaux."[10]

His good reputation growing in the community at large, Burnham gained further esteem among his Thibodaux in-laws not too long after his marriage to Clementine Braud. His mother-in-law, Marie Felicité Trahan Braud, died in the summer of 1842, and Burnham served as administrator of her succession, a recognition that Burnham had settled into the life of and was making a respectable living in Thibodaux.[11]

Specific evidence of Burnham's construction projects appears in 1844 and 1845. On March 11, 1844, Burnham contracted with a mercantile company, Lacapère & Montagnan, to build "a house between his [Lacapère's] brick store and Cole's office"[12] sized about thirty-six feet long by twenty feet deep. The house would enclose a space between the store and office and was intended to serve as "three apartments [and] an office with chimney." A door opened into a sleeping room, "which will also have a door opening into the yard. In the third room there will be a door and two windows." The requisite brick front was planned to resemble the brick used on the adjoining store, and Burnham was directed to build "a gallery on the model of that of B. F. Holden," surrounding the entire property of the client. He agreed to furnish brick, liming sand, and labor and to plaster the exterior and interior, including the wall of Cole's office, and paint inside and out, including the gallery. Lacapère took on the provision of "scantling and plank" he had on-site and from the sawmill of Townsend and Foley, as well as locks and fasteners for doors on the front. For the work, Lacapère contracted to pay Burnham $480.

A job dispute and suit arose between the parties, apparently because Burnham was asked to do more than had been contracted. In October 1844 the Second Judicial District Court judge, Louis Bush, appointed two "experts," William Mooney for the claimants and, illustrating Burnham's close connection with him, Absalom Kees for Burnham, to work out the details. Burnham ended up collecting $524.44, but the amount was debited $167.71, "for work omitted to be done as per Contract together with allowances for work not done in a Workman Like manner."[13]

Burnham was sued again and settled a claim for $23.50 in contract wages for labor accomplished over a time of two years by John McClellan, a mason. McClellan worked on Burnham's own "new house next to Dr. Scudday," the

Burnham house then an impressive brick structure "23½ feet high." In addition, McClellan claimed $0.75 wages for himself; $1.75 for 3½ days' work by McClelland and one Jas. Inneus "laying 2 hearths;" unspecified wages for one day's work by two hired masons at J. Bernard's home located "below Thibodaux on Bayou Terrebonne;" $18.00 for "building one chimney and pillars for him [Burnham] in the house of J. B. Bernard;" and an amount for "building 4 pillars in his house," that cost $1.00. The tall "new house" that Burnham constructed adjoining Dr. James Scudday seems to have been attached to the rear of the Burnham residence and may have been part of the family's kitchen, a shop, and/or living quarters for workers.[14]

Although E. T. Burnham at first relied upon his apprentices and contracted labor, by the middle of the 1840s he commenced buying enslaved workers. The initial arrangements were intended to supply domestic servants, as in the acquisition of Betsy, "age 12 or 13," on May 13, 1845. Burnham paid $525 to Richard Lawless of Kentucky for the young girl in a sale, witnessed by the prominent businessmen James Frost and Richard G. Darden. He financed the purchase of Betsy through a mortgage both on her and on his property located on lot 42 on the 1842 Grinage plat. Delphine Burnham likely needed Betsy to help with their growing family, which by 1845 included a son, Edward, a daughter, Sarah, and a newborn, Julia. Although Betsy at first may have proved helpful, she was sold in 1847 for $500. In January 1853, Burnham then acquired another enslaved woman, she too named Betsy. The acquisition included her three small children and one girl named "Kitty," sixteen years old and described as a "mulatress." Burnham purchased all through a well-known Missouri-based dealer named John R. White, and all originated out of state. Only two months later, Betsy and her children were sold to William A. Shaffer for $1,300 cash. Betsy again returned to the Burnham family in 1855, when Shaffer sold her back for $1,400.[15] Kitty may have remained with the Burnhams as their house servant.

Most of E. T. Burnham's acquisitions, however, were for enslaved artisans who could assist in his carpentry work. The Lafourche Parish clerk of court records for them begin in 1849 and continue through the mid-1850s, mainly as purchases, but sometimes Burnham sold the artisans to others in the community. For example, the "agricultural firm of Blanchard and Ransom" bought from Burnham a man named Henry in January 1853, for $1,100; Thibodaux resident John C. Regan (Frost's father-in-law) acquired the man, Bob, in April 1856, also for $1,100.[16]

IMAGE 21. Guion Academy, c. 1910. Courtesy of Nicholls State University Archives.

What appears to be Burnham's first major public building job was the Guion Academy, completed in 1849. Constructed on land donated by George S. Guion, on the west side of Jackson Street at its corner with Clinton Street (now West Tenth Street), it backed up to Harrison Street. The Guion Academy remained as a major landmark in the town until the early 1900s, replaced by the Thibodaux High School on East Seventh Street beyond the south corner of Goode Street, in the southern outskirts of Thibodaux. That building still exists but is now a public elementary school. The two Jackson Street lots on which the Guion Academy stood are now a public park.

Discussions regarding the new school on Jackson began in the town council well before any school construction contract could be considered. For a long time, the town fathers had viewed the absence of a decent public school as a great hindrance to the community's well-being. Finally, in early 1847 the council acted. As with any such public contract in antebellum Thibodaux, personal and business relationships made a difference. Both of Burnham's trade peers, Absalom Kees and Morgan Springer, held posts on the council at various times in the mid- to late 1840s, and by that time Burnham was a well-established builder in the larger community, living and working amid fellow artisans along and near Jackson and the corner of

St. Mary. Unlike several of them, he seems not to have sought out public office with the town government. The proximity of the Burnham shop and residence to the Union Bank of Louisiana also opened up close acquaintance between Burnham and the bank's directors, including Guion. And as noted above, Burnham and his family were members of the town's First Methodist Church, which numerous valued business contacts attended.

In early March 1847, Burnham received a contract to erect "a [brick] school house according to plans and specifications at B. F. Holden's store," for $2,800. A bid from Arthur M. Foley and Sumner Townsend for $4,500 (or if constructed in wood, $3,500) lost out. Burnham had a choice of using slate or wood shingles for the school. But the job could not proceed as planned, and at the May meeting of the council Burnham withdrew his first proposition and presented an alternate (unrecorded) one. There, the project came to a halt.[17]

The town government determined that it needed permission from the state legislature to establish "a distinct and separate school district" in the incorporated town. When the issue was resolved by July 13, 1848, the trustees selected a set of building plans by the firm of Springer and Frost, not by Burnham, for the "School House." Its cost could not exceed $3,000. A building committee was appointed to superintend the construction. But, changing course, the council then determined to contract with Edward T. Burnham—Springer's position on the council had created a conflict of interest. Dated July 24, 1848, the contract required Burnham to construct a two-story brick building fifty feet long by thirty-two feet wide. Its ground floor would have eleven-foot ceilings and be supplied with desks, the second story to have ceilings twelve feet clear. When finished on March 10, 1849, the school building cost $2,980. Burnham received an additional $90 for materials and labor for "hanging sash to the windows," and the council asked him to construct two privies as well as a rear shed "the length of the house, twelve feet wide . . . to protect the cisterns from exposure to the weather."[18]

The town's decision to build and tax its citizens for a school was not entirely popular, and the school's large size relative to the town's child population came under criticism. Although figures are unstated, the school supporters advised the council that the growth of the school-age population, only 124 in the 1840 Census, now required a structure of the size as designed and built. During the Civil War, the academy was occupied by United States Colored Troops, who remained until late 1865. The Guion Academy eventually resumed its public-school functions. Its attendees were white students only.[19]

In early 1850 Burnham sold two portions of his home lot on the corner of Jackson and St. Bridget. The first fronted fifty feet on St. Bridget by seventy feet in depth, with "a brick kitchen in the rear of the said lot to be the boundary lines in its rear." The buyers, Mrs. Cyrus F. Moulton and Miss Seeyminda Burton, paid $1,100. The second sale, to Jacob Webre (or Weber), was of fifty feet front on Jackson by 171 feet deep, behind or east of which the Scudday property was located. Situated further to the south and west along Jackson was the Lacapère lot on which Burnham had worked six years prior. The sales left Burnham with a tract of 121 feet front on Jackson at St. Bridget. His residence remained facing Jackson, and he kept his business address on St. Bridget.[20] In April 1854 Burnham sold the rest of his Thibodaux property to James F. Thompson,[21] and in July Burnham readied his family to move to a farm in Terrebonne Parish about three miles south of Thibodaux and fronting on Bayou Terrebonne. The farm was close to Terrebonne Station and to important Winder and Armitage families. The new Burnham family tract measured 1½ arpents in width and twenty arpents deep. Of the $2,500 total cost, Burnham paid $700 down and was clear of the remaining $1,800 debt within a year.[22]

What could have prompted the Burnham family to leave the growing, prosperous town of Thibodaux? Although lacking direct evidence, one can see that a number of factors played a part. We know that between 1845 and 1860, in addition to Edward, Sarah, and Julia, the Burnhams welcomed more children. The Census of 1860 lists Thomas, age ten, and Catherine, age six, Elliot, age four, and a baby girl, Louisa (or Delphine), age one.[23] Burnham's wife Lucy died in 1859, probably from complications in giving birth to Louisa. Thus, the Burnham family had outgrown the home on Jackson Street. In addition, concerns of safety after the terrible yellow fever epidemic of 1853 in Thibodaux helped determine Burnham to move. Perhaps as well, and like so many in Louisiana, Burnham may have decided that taking on a farm represented a step up in society. Finally, as local newspapers noted, the part of the town in which the Burnhams resided was near to a number of taverns and must have been dirty and noisy from traffic and other activity. When Lucy Delphine Burnham's succession inventory was taken in 1863, the Burnham farm was connected to Martha Grundy Winder (Ducros Plantation) on the Bayou Terrebonne's right-descending bank; it was bordered above (toward Thibodaux) by the property of Marlbrough & Lajaunie. Among the movables in the community property, her succession contained various farm implements, Burnham's carpenter tools, bench, and tool chests, and house furnishings, books, and pictures. Land prices were adversely affected by the Civil War, and the lot received a value of $582.00; the land and physical residence were given a combined value of only $1,500.[24] At a meeting on March 27, 1863, the family determined to sell everything for the appraisal total of $2,082.[25] None of the Burnham family is listed in the 1860 Census in Lafourche Parish, and by 1870, they all had disappeared from Terrebonne Parish too.[26]

Did E. T. Burnham, in 1854 established as a planter, continue in his building trade? The answer is definitely—and in a historically decisive way. The story again involves St. John's Episcopal Church, which Burnham's friends Absalom Kees and James Frost had constructed in 1843 and 1844.

By the early 1850s St. John's was what might be called "depressed." The church's longtime leader, Bishop Leonidas Polk, experienced financial difficulties after cholera decimated his enslaved laborers in 1849 and a tornado demolished the Leighton Plantation sugar mill and worker cabins in 1850. In 1854, Polk turned over the plantation to creditors and moved to New Orleans. A much-loved priest at St. John's, John Sandels, resigned in 1850, and the two others hired from 1850 to 1853 each remained in Thibodaux only a year. Between December 1852 and March 1854, the church had no full-time rector. During the interval, the congregation was caught in the four-month-long yellow fever epidemic that arrived during the 1853 summer. The epidemic rocked the countryside and towns from Thibodaux to Donaldsonville at the Mississippi River. Many families of St. John's lost relatives and friends. The hire of Marylander Reverend Thomas R. B. Trader in 1854, however, heralded beneficial change for St. John's, and the congregation expressed its interest in renovating the church building. Among its many problems, the roof leaked, the front door opening from the portico into the seating area allowed cold air directly into the church, and the heating system was old and inadequate.[27]

Almost simultaneous with these events at St. John's, in 1855 and 1856, the New Orleans architect Henry Howard had been working near Labadieville, supervising a house construction for Oakwood Plantation owner P. Lansdale Cox, a native of New York. Cox undoubtedly persuaded St. John's, of which he was a vestry member and strong supporter, to employ Howard in planning changes for the church. The result was a building contract with Thibodaux's Connecticut Yankee, E. T. Burnham, signed on June 11, 1856, to renovate

Images 22 and 23. Turpin carpenter's chest, c. 1850. Exterior view with closed chest (*above*) and open chest showing tools (*below*). Courtesy of the Louisiana State Museum, gift of William P. O'Shea and Joseph R. Berrigan, 12802.

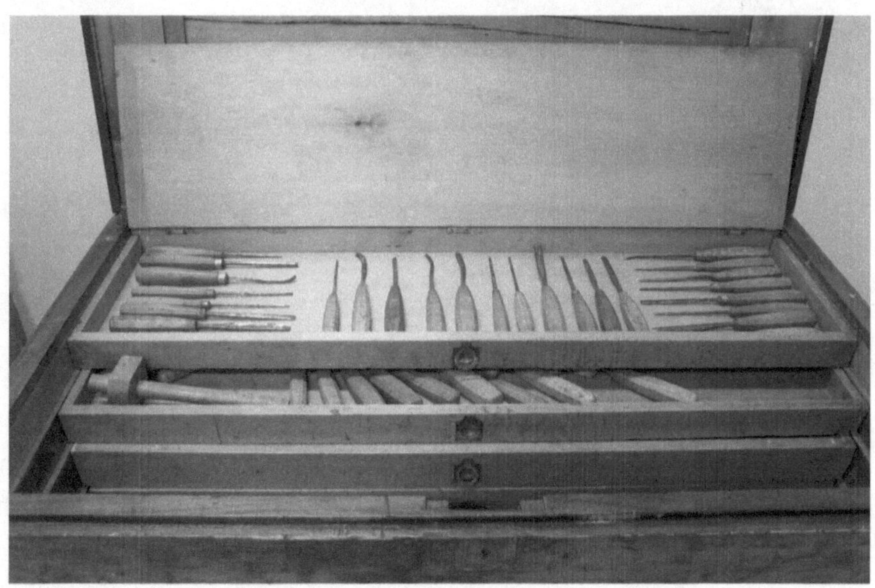

St. John's. Howard designed the "alterations, additions, and repairs" and prepared the specifications that made up the building agreement. The contract specified in detail what Burnham must do and, in many cases, how to do it and where materials were to be obtained. The Morgan's Louisiana and Texas railroad, available at both Lafourche Crossing and Terrebonne Station, gave easy access to the New Orleans lumberyards, special stores, and foundries, and thus, to eastern-made goods. Like the 1861 Lafourche Parish courthouse designed by Howard, the variety and complexity of work required numerous artisans. The margins of the beautifully written and recorded St. John's contract contain helpful, simply worded guides to design and building elements such as the "Doorway," "Pews," "Lectern Pulpit," and "Furnace." Such notations emphasized to and reminded Burnham and the building committee what must be accomplished. The committee obligated St. John's to pay Burnham $3,350 on November 1, 1856, the date set "for the completion of the building."[28]

IMAGE 24. During a 1990s St. John's Episcopal Church renovation, the 1856 bench seats were removed for repairs. Tucked up and well-hidden under the corner of a rear seat was a pair of worn worker's shoes; they had remained in place for about 140 years, perhaps following an old European and northeast United States good-luck tradition of hiding shoes in buildings.[29] Or, maybe hiding the shoes of a fellow worker provided only a practical joke. Photo by Clifton Theriot.

At this time, Burnham was staffed with enslaved artisans, among them one named Bob, newly purchased in 1854. Assuming that the four artisans he acquired in 1849–1850 still worked for him, he was well supplied with qualified laborers. They—along with other workers whom Burnham leased, and with independent contractors like masons, painters, and plasterers, and their own laborers—could handle much of the work at St. John's. The nearby sawmill, as well, carried many items that had not been available in 1843 and 1844. Regrettably, no photographic record, ledger, or diary of the event was preserved. Like the first church construction in 1843, the scene was busy and rather hazardous. Both outer and inner work required scaffolding; the rebuilding of the church façade was especially tricky, involving careful bracing of the church pediment before and during removal of the four columns. In place of the old portico, Burnham had to erect a front brick wall with good foundations, the wall to be formed carefully in order to support the pediment and bell tower and to hold two tall, Roman-style arched windows and a handsome sliding front door. Known as a "pocket door," it opened into the new vestibule. The wall at the Jackson Street end of the nave was set forward a few feet to provide more seating, and new copper gutters were installed. Repairs and reinforcements were made to the belfry to accommodate the heavy new bell from Meneely's Bell Foundry in West Troy, New York. Funds for the bell had been given to St. John's by Marcus Zills, a prominent Thibodaux merchant who died in 1853. The bell was erected temporarily on a stand near the rear of the church. The church floors from 1844 were replaced with "new yellow pine well-dressed planks not over five inches wide" and defect-free. The box pews of the 1843–1844 St. John's gave way to bench pews "newly fitted up (without doors)," and "the seats to be made easy and comfortable, each pew to have a proper kneeling stool." A significant feature in the vestibule was the winding stairway leading to the new "Gallery for Choir." It cut across the view from one of the tall front windows and was an especially typical, lovely element of Howard's design. The stairway may have been created in Burnham's shop, but the "fancy turned" newel, balusters, and handrail made of black walnut may have been sent south from the eastern United States.[30]

Significant changes also took place to improve heating, for which the building committee furnished "a warm air furnace with all necessary pipes and registers the same as shall be built in brickwork and put in good working order." To assist with air circulation an "enriched iron ventilator and enriched centre flowers round it, finished in an appropriate and workman-like manner" were planned for the middle of the church ceiling. The specifications required that all the tall, double-hung windows allow for opening to fresh air. Many of the classical features from the 1844 church were kept, such as the Greek key framing around church windows and doors, and some were added in the new construction. This created a mix of visual elements that can be termed Classical Revival style.[31]

Certain elements of the church renovation may have resulted from the anticipated "omissions, additions, and alteration of the plans."[32] The existing pew half-kneelers and visible evidence of two chimneys, not just one, raise the question. Then again, later renovations took place. For example, a recess chancel and the main walls and ceiling lined with bead-cut boards placed on

IMAGE 25. St. John's Episcopal Church, c. 1880.
Courtesy of Nicholls State University Archives

IMAGE 26. Henry Howard, 1855.
Courtesy of Historic New Orleans Collection, accession no. 2005.0069.23.

atop old walls—instead of restored plastered walls and ceiling—appeared after the Civil War. In the 1930s, a stained-glass window of St. John the Evangelist, created by the noted artist Charles Connick of Boston, was installed above the altar by the New Orleans architect Richard Koch. Electric lighting, natural gas, and air conditioning and heating were added during the mid- to late twentieth century. St. John's otherwise retains much from the 1856 renovation. The seating is the same, the choir gallery is there, the belfry and the tall windows have survived hurricanes, and the street façade remains, except for new steps and a landing added in the 1990s. It feels like the 1856 church: St. John's partly remains Edward Truman Burnham's creation.

Another major opportunity for Burnham came about even as the St. John's renovation proceeded. For some years, Thibodaux had relied upon ferry service located at the head of Maronge Street to cross Bayou Lafourche. By the 1850s, the ferry provided slow, inconvenient travel to and from the increasingly populous bayou bank opposite to the town. Town investors realized the promise of personal profit from having a decent toll bridge and formed the Thibodaux Bridge Company. Officially enabled by the passage of a law at the state level, the town government financially supported the bridge, and the bridge company's stock subscribers were major community leaders. The New Orleans engineering firm of Bayley & Nelson completed the new bridge plans and made them available for inspection at the local post office on April 19, 1856. By midsummer 1856, the bridge company readied to bid the work for a pivot bridge to be located "at any suitable point, within the [town] limits" over which, "at any time of the day or the night, any person or persons, horses, mules, cattle, carts, wagons, carriages of all kinds, and all other vehicles of whatsoever nature, empty or loaded," might cross.[33]

The bridge company contracted with E. T. Burnham on August 1, 1856, "to build and complete a draw bridge . . . across Bayou Lafourche at Thibodaux," its site to be at the head of Jackson Street. Burnham was obligated to complete the work by June 16, 1857, for which he agreed to receive $22,000 in installments. Soon after the signing, Burnham dealt with the local foundry, P. H. Gary & Co. (Patrick H. Gary personally serving on the bridge company board of directors), for "furnishing of all the wrought iron and cast iron" for the bridge. Sumner Townsend, an owner of the local sawmill, became surety for Burnham in the original contract.[34]

Work quickly began, its progress reported in the *New Orleans Crescent*, citing *The Thibodaux Minerva*:

> Mr. E. T. Burnham, contractor of the Thibodaux bridge, commenced operations on Monday last. He has already constructed a shop for his workmen, and will commence the foundation of the pillars at an early day. Weather permitting, the bridge will be completed by March next.[35]

But delays occurred, and by February 1857 an extensive contract modification was required. A new completion date was set for September 16, and Burnham was allowed to drive the "approach and guard piles" when "water in the bayou Lafourche" rose. The $6,000 payment due him on June 16 would take place at the new time of completion. New schedules for payments were arranged, and the parties revised particulars for iron delivery dates. Soon, however, Burnham decided not to continue. He transferred to Sumner Townsend all the obligations and consideration set forth in the original and subsequent agreements as well as all the wood, brick, and other materials already acquired and gave Townsend a note for $1,000. Townsend agreed to pay Burnham's debts for work and materials, the wages of two enslaved people of the Lafourche and Terrebonne Navigation Company, an amount due "Frost's estate for wages of a negro," the wages of four white laborers, and an amount due to one "Wm J. Potavint" for lumber. Finally, Townsend gave Burnham a note for $490 in favor of Foley and Townsend, co-owners of the sawmill.[36] (The Poitevent family still owns timberland in St. Tammany Parish.)[37]

The record is dark about reasons for Burnham's sudden change. But it may be no coincidence that Burnham—evidently in need of money—on February 4, 1857, sold the planter William A. Shaffer an enslaved man named Peter, age thirty, his twenty-five-year-old wife Frances, and their child of twelve months, all for $6,200; and again, two weeks later, for $1,600 Burnham sold Shaffer an enslaved woman named Elizabeth, age thirty, and her three children, ages ten, six, and four. There is no evidence of Burnham undertaking additional building in or around Thibodaux, and he apparently concentrated thereafter on farming.[38]

Edward Truman Burnham's contributions to the Thibodaux landscape since his arrival in the 1830s were both wondrous and lasting. The building of the Guion Academy provided citizens with a much-needed educational improvement. Since its founding in 1820, Thibodaux had relied upon occasional, short-lived academies for basic school instruction. The Guion Academy remained functional for more than sixty years, until replaced by a modern public high school at the east end of Seventh Street; that "new" school building continues use as an elementary school. And the architectural renovations conducted at St. John's Episcopal Church have endured to the present time, through a civil war, epidemics, the Great Depression, and two world wars.

Epilogue

This history has concentrated on the lives of six master carpenters who spent many of their productive years in antebellum Thibodaux and the three adjacent parishes of Lafourche, Assumption, and Terrebonne. Of those builders, James Frost died of yellow fever in November 1853, and Morgan Springer died in August 1861, soon after the Civil War began.

We now complete the stories of Absalom Kees, Edward T. Burnham, Sciotha S. Evans, and John Bellsen, set mainly during and after the Civil War.

Absalom Kees

Living near Lockport on Sawmill Plantation following his departure from Thibodaux, Kees pursued at least one side-occupation in addition to sugarcane farming. With two others, Benjamin Parker and Gustave Arbribat, in the mid-1850s Kees ran a ferry from the town of Lockport over to the left descending bank of Bayou Lafourche. In September 1858 they received permission from the parish government to auction their right to keep the ferry.[1] Kees was also active in the local chapter of the anti-Roman Catholic, anti-immigrant political party known as the American Party, popularly referred to as the Know-Nothing Party. Kees's fellows included such prominent Thibodaux citizens as Patrick H. Gary, Richardson G. Darden, and Jonah H. White. They represented Lafourche at the American Party convention in Baton Rouge in June 1857.[2]

By the time that the Civil War commenced, Absalom Kees had sold off portions of his large Sawmill Plantation to neighbors and to his Meegel in-law relatives, Edward and Frederick. His death came in the fall of 1863, in his seventy-fourth year. As described in testimonies for his formal succession proceedings, Kees died as he returned alone from a trip that had taken him first to Thibodaux, then to Houma. For his route home from Terrebonne Parish, instead of retracing his way, Kees decided upon a shortcut through the marshes and the two freshwater bodies, Lake Long and Lake Fields, that separated Bayou Terrebonne from the Bayou Lafourche ridge. In order to accomplish his trip, Kees borrowed a small "hunting pirogue." Witnesses saw Kees depart, paddling the pirogue. Relatives and others who had been with him before his trip depicted Kees as a "tall man, but very thin" and in poor physical and mental health. Somewhere during his paddle trip through the marshes and lakes he either fell overboard or the pirogue flipped. The small pirogue was recovered months later, but Kees's body was never found. Several people who testified also noted that when Kees set out, the weather was especially cold and windy, minimizing any chance of survival for someone in Kees's poor health. The existence of an active war in the area and a consequential lack of rescue facilities and personnel meant that few people were available to search for the old master carpenter.[3]

Edward T. Burnham

At the time of the 1860 Census in Terrebonne Parish's Ward 1, E. T. Burnham lived near Terrebonne Station at dwelling number 880. Listed with him were seven children, E[dward], age twenty; Sarah, seventeen; Julia, fifteen; Thomas, nine; Catherine, six; Elliot, four; and Louisa, age one. However, the census taker had made one mistake: according to family records, "Elliot" was in fact a girl, Ellen Maria, born in 1856. Burnham's wife, Delphine, was absent from the count. She had died September 22, 1859, perhaps from the effects of a difficult birth of her namesake, Louisa Delphine Burnham, the previous May 26.[4]

The family did not remain in their home for long. Roderick Burnham, a Burnham family chronicler and genealogist living in New England in the 1860s, depicted E. T. Burnham in 1860 as supportive of the Democratic Party and its presidential candidate Stephen A. Douglas. Burnham opposed Louisiana's secession from the United States. When war erupted and the Federal Navy blockaded the Mississippi River entrance from the Gulf of Mexico, he encouraged his son Edward to join the Union fleet. After the navy's arrival in New Orleans in the spring of 1862 and General Benjamin Butler's call for citizens to support the US Constitution and laws, E. T. Burnham made his way to New Orleans and pledged his allegiance to the Union cause. Upon his return to Terrebonne, Burnham encountered threats of injury and arrest from Confederate sympathizers, who intimidated any and all Union supporters. Avoiding arrest, Burnham became a Union Army scout with the Eighth Vermont Volunteers and later for Brigadier General Godfrey Weitzel when his forces invaded Bayou Lafourche in the autumn of 1862.[5]

Before the spring of 1863, the family had sold their farm and home in Terrebonne Parish. A number of Burnham's daughters were taken in by relatives and friends living near Hartford, Connecticut.[6] Burnham remained in New Orleans, where he joined the Union Army as part of the Department of the Gulf. He was commissioned in September 1863 and made captain of the Fourth Regiment, Engineers, Corps d'Afrique; it soon was renamed Company F, Ninety-Eighth Regiment, US Colored Infantry.[7] The Union Army Department of the Gulf constructed and oversaw numerous posts, fortifications, stockades, and camps in the Lafourche District. The encampments and fortifications were located mainly along and near the New Orleans, Opelousas, and Great Western Railroad between Algiers on the west bank of the Mississippi River, across from New Orleans, and Brashear City on the Atchafalaya River. For the remainder of the war, Burnham's Company F was active with work on the railroad or in army installations. By 1865, Burnham had sickened, suffering from "rheumatic pains and stiffness," partial deafness, and bad eyesight. Receiving a medical certificate showing his inability to continue in service, Burnham was discharged June 13, 1865.[8]

Burnham's chronology after his military discharge is unclear. He may have traveled to Connecticut to rejoin the children who had moved to New England and chose to remain awhile rather than return to a still-turbulent Louisiana. At some stage, he settled in New Iberia, on Bayou Teche, where son Thomas (1850–1949) lived and worked as a builder-contractor. Finding politics to his interest during the Reconstruction years, Burnham joined the Liberal Republican Party of Iberia Parish. In May 1872, he was chosen to be an Iberia Parish Republican Party delegate to the state party convention in New Orleans; its chairman was P. B. S. Pinchback, Louisiana's lieutenant governor, soon to become governor.[9] Burnham died in New Orleans in August 1878, and he was buried in Rosehill Cemetery in New Iberia.[10]

John Bellsen

In 1860, John Bellsen lived near his in-laws in Marksville, Avoyelles Parish, where he prospered as operator of a lumber establishment (or lumber mill). After the Civil War, Bellsen returned to his old occupation of growing sugarcane. As of the 1870 Census, the Bellsen real estate holdings were valued at $5,000. At the time, he and his wife Sarah were parents of two girls, Lelia (1865) and Caroline (1867);[11] and in 1873 Sarah gave birth to a son, Vedder, in Baton Rouge.[12] Still residing in Avoyelles in 1885, the family prepared to leave Louisiana, and in June of that year Bellsen offered to sell the plantation and sugar mill, together with "cows, horses, oxen, wagons, etc.," in an auction.[13]

For reasons unknown, the Bellsens were destined for Garland, Texas, near Dallas. There, Bellsen would remain well past the 1889 marriage of his daughter, Lee (Lelia), to a dentist named Eugenious Horton McCoy.[14] A final move came around 1894, probably to be near to Lee's family, when John and Sarah Elizabeth Bellsen resettled for a final time to Beeville, Texas, north of Corpus Christi. John Bellsen, the builder of the Assumption and Lafourche Parish jails and of St. Matthew's Episcopal Church in Houma in the 1850s, died on October 23, 1897, and is buried in Evergreen Cemetery, Beeville.[15]

Sciotha S. Evans

Sciotha Evans and his family retained their St. Mary Street property in Thibodaux until he moved back to Missouri in the late 1880s. After the Civil War, apparently having avoided taking sides in the conflict, Evans acquired an ownership interest in the Thibodaux sawmill. The mill was then located not far above Church Street—and the site of the original mill built by Absalom Kees—and sold to Arthur M. Foley. The company's property at that time included forest land in Franklin Parish, perhaps to ensure a supply for the mill.[16] In debt, Evans disposed of his Thibodaux Saw Mill Company stock and interests in the mill and timber land in 1869.[17]

In November 1870 Mary Jane Evans, Sciotha's Kentucky-born wife, died. A woman "possessed of all the elements of kindness, gentleness, and Christian humility," in the eyes of the editor of *The Weekly Thibodaux Sentinel*, her passing was due to a "peculiar epidemic" that "has reaped a rich harvest in this parish during the present year."[18] Mary Jane Elam Evans was buried in St. John's Episcopal Church Cemetery in Thibodaux.[19]

By 1880, at the age of fifty-seven and still practicing carpentry, Evans resided on St. Mary Street with three daughters: Maggie, age twenty-four and a "domestic"; Julia, age twenty-two, occupation "keep[ing] house"; and Fanny, twenty, "at home." The oldest daughter, Eudora, no longer lived with them.[20] On March 4, 1886, Evans sold the family home, shop, and lot to John McCulla for $900 cash and returned to Center, Call County, Missouri, the community from which he had come in the late 1840s.[21] Sciotha S. Evans died there on January 30, 1899, and was interred in the Salem Cemetery.[22]

***

Craftsmen in carpentry and associated skills were much in demand in antebellum southern Louisiana, nowhere more so than alongside Bayous Lafourche and Terrebonne. There, a plantation economy developed after 1815, at first mainly based on cotton agriculture, but soon, growing and processing sugarcane. Steamboats and, eventually, railroad transportation to and from the area arrived. Steam-driven mills and foundries were built, and they required specially trained labor; housing needs were great, especially on the larger sugarcane plantations and in and around towns like Houma and Thibodaux.

Notably, after about 1830, ample credit from newly formed regional banks financed the acquisition of land and improvements, and immigration from other states and abroad supplied workers. Enslaved persons were brought in, mainly from other southern and border states, to work in the fields and mills. The introduction of the American system of human bondage into the Bayou Lafourche area promoted trading in enslaved people, financed largely through the readily available credit from regional banks. Tragically, holding and trafficking in enslaved people produced even more wealth.

As the population alongside Bayous Lafourche and Terrebonne grew and wealth increased, the region demanded skilled workers. This included carpenters, joiners, masons, painters, plasterers, and associated building trades, as well as foundrymen, boilermakers, and other metalwork occupations. Importantly, those craftsmen trained their bonded workers to become artisans in many such callings.

The arrival in Thibodaux and vicinity of our six master carpenters occurred roughly between 1828 and 1847. Anglo-Americans all, they came from a variety of places and backgrounds in New England, New York, western Pennsylvania, the Midwest, and the southern Appalachians. All had experience and skills in European and early American traditional woodworking and to some degree in brick and stone masonry. Absalom Kees also became known as an "engineer," from his background in water-powered grain milling, steam-driven cotton ginning, and steam-powered sugarcane and saw milling. By all evidence, the master carpenters came to Bayou Lafourche as literate, well-schooled men. Each craftsman was soon able to cultivate and use political, social, and economic connections in his parish and town, and several of them became local political leaders. All joined the new Protestant churches, some of them helping to found and build the first ones in Thibodaux and Houma. There is little indication that they traveled long distances out of the region for work or were away for long periods; Bayou Lafourche country supplied plentiful employment.

Among the master carpenters, only Burnham is recorded apprenticing White helpers. All the builders eventually relied not only upon White, Caucasian workers (such as those recorded at Ducros Plantation) but enslaved men of African heritage to train and use as carpenters and joiners. Their knowledge and experience were invaluable. Enslaved women were bought especially for and worked as domestic help in the builders' homes. The details of the lives and work of men and women held in servitude in the town of Thibodaux deserve more study. Some enslaved artisans (and notably enslaved domestics) were given special treatment—in some cases, even manumission—by their slaveholders.

The later career of E. T. Burnham seems unique: he alone among the master carpenters allied with one or the other side in the Civil War. Burnham favored the Union cause, joining it in 1863, and one child, Thomas Burnham, joined the US Navy. Most of the rest of his family was forced to flee the bayou country. Following the war, Burnham actively supported Radical Reconstruction in south Louisiana.

When Absalom Kees stepped off a boat in Thibodaux in 1828, the building trades had barely been exposed to mechanization, industrial methods, and factory-made materials. As described in the book *White Pillars* by the architectural historian J. Frazer Smith, at the time of Kees's arrival structural timbers still "were hewn, jointed, and pegged" using hand tools, and "carpenters . . . made the sash, frames, panels, chimney pieces, doors, and cabinets, all right there on the job."[23] For many years, there were no professionally trained architects to direct the builders; any such information came from published builder manuals, or from "builders' rule of thumb practices."[24] The building contracts for St. John's in 1843 and in 1856, and those for the Assumption and Lafourche Parish jails in the 1850s and for the Lafourche Parish courthouse in 1859–1861, all reveal that the passage of time, changes in technology, and closer connections with New Orleans had produced a much-elevated level of sophistication in building design, materials, and methods and tools of construction. This was especially so after the New Orleans architect Henry Howard commenced working in the Lafourche area. Howard also may have brought to the Lafourche country some of what the scholar S. Frederick Starr noted were "early manifestations of what would become a basic feature of American life: its startling impermanence."[25]

The master carpenters whom we have explored lived in a transitory age, leading to machine-driven production. J. Frazer Smith observed that after 1840 the presence of steam planing mills in communities like Thibodaux allowed for "planed lumber and moldings, sash and doors, and joiner work of many kinds."[26] The master carpenters remained craftsmen and architects in wood, using special, wooden-handled implements for jobs that they undertook, each owning his valuable tool chests; but they were challenged in new ways. Eric Sloane described the early American craftsman as having owned tools that "might appear pathetically poor, but his ways were honest and lasting and beautiful to an extent that is today deemed over and above requirements."[27]

The master builders of antebellum Lafourche displayed an honest and lasting quality in their creations, of which too few exist today. Preserving buildings that remain from the nineteenth and early twentieth centuries is a goal worthy of the craftsmen and others who helped design and build them. Every such creation has a story that is part of the complex matrix of American life, surely and notably in the Lafourche country of Louisiana. Each was, in some ways, an example of prideful joy in work, in which all of America participated and from which everyone benefited. The spirit was expressed by Walt Whitman, in *Leaves of Grass,* "I Hear America Singing":

I hear America singing, the varied carols I hear,

Those of mechanics, each one singing his as it should be blithe and strong,

The carpenter singing as he measures his plank or beam,

The mason singing his as he makes ready for work, or leaves off work,

The boatman singing what belongs to him in his boat, the deckhand singing on the steamboat deck,

The shoemaker singing as he sits on his bench, the hatter singing as he stands,

The wood-cutter's song, the ploughboy's on his way in the morning, or at noon intermission or at sundown,

The delicious singing of the mother, or of the young wife at work, or of the girl sewing or washing,

Each singing what belongs to him or her and to none else,

The day what belongs to the day–at night the party of young fellows, robust, friendly,

Singing with open mouths their strong melodious songs.[28]

Appendix

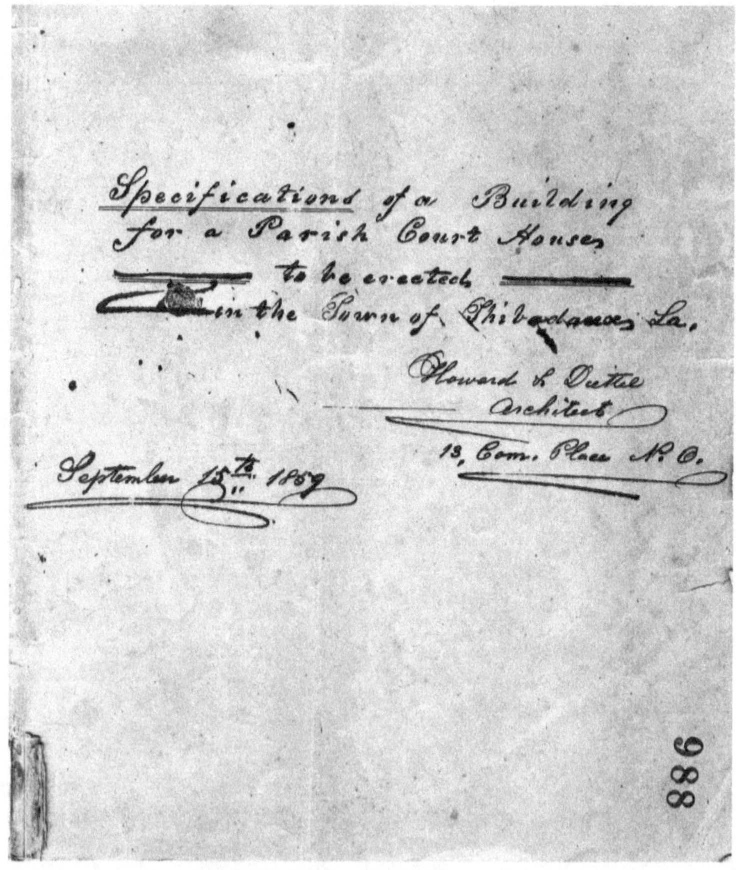

Specifications of a Building
for a Parish Court House
to be erected
in the Town of Thibodaux La.

Howard & Diettel
Architects

13, Com. Place N.O.

September 15th 1859

886

Specifications of a Building for a Parish Court House to be erected in the town of Thibodaux, La.

Howard and Diettel Architects
13, Com. Place N.O.

September 15, 1859

Photos courtesy of Nicholls State University Archives

F

Specifications of a building for a Parish Court House to be erected on a certain Square of ground situated in the Town of Thibodaux Parish of Lafourche La. (under the direction of a Superintendent appointed by the building committee for that purpose according to the accompanying plans, elevations and sections designed and prepared by Howard & Diettel architects, and agreeably to such further drawings and directions in explanation thereof, as may be furnished therefor, from time to time. ——————

—— The size of the building, its height, the height of stories, and other parts; the thickness of walls, dimensions, divisions, and subdivisions, and the arrangement and details of the building, are to be the same as set forth and shown on the several drawings; all the measurements being in English feet and inches, and where not figured to be measured by the scale of the drawing as given thereon.

Bricklayers' Work.

Trenches. —— The trenches for the footings under walls shall be dug to the required widths and 18 inches deep below the present surface of the grounds, their bottoms to be made level, hard and solid, to receive the brickwork without planks. ——————

—— The trenches for the foundations under the front columns shall be dug 8 feet square and 2 feet 6 inches deep below the surface of the ground, the bottom to be made solid and covered with two thicknesses of sound 2 inch Cypress planks laid crossing one another. ——————

—— After the foundations are put in, the trenches shall be filled up with proper earth and rammed down in a solid manner. ——

—— —— The ground round the outside of the building shall be filled up so as to conceal the upper offset of the footings and graded out from the walls and Portico for the width of 20 feet, with a gradual descent down to the present surface of the ground. ——————

Specifications of a building for a Parish Court House to be erected on a certain square of ground situated in the town of Thibodaux Parish of Lafourche La. (under the direction of a Superintendent appointed by the building committee for that purpose according to the accompanying plans, elevations and sections designed and prepared by Howard and Diettel architects, and agreeably to such further drawings and directions in explanation thereof, as may be furnished therefor, from time to time. ____________________

__________ The size of the building, its height, the height of stories, and other parts; the thickness of walls, dimensions, divisions, and subdivisions, and the arrangement and details of the building, are to be the same as set forth and shown on the several drawings; all the measurements being in English feet and inches, and where not figured to be measured by the scale of the drawing as given thereon.

Bricklayers' Work

Trenches. ——————

The trenches for the footings under walls shall be dug to the required widths and 18 inches deep below the present surface of the ground, their bottoms to be made level, hard and solid, to receive the brickwork without planks. __________

__________ The trenches for the foundations under the front columns shall be dug 8 feet square and 2 feet 6 inches deep below the surface of the ground, the bottom to be made solid, and covered with two thicknesses of sound 2 inch Cypress planks laid crossing one another. ________________

________________ After the foundations are put in, the trenches shall be filled up with proper earth and rammed down in a solid manner. _________

__________________________ The ground round the outside of the building shall be filled up so as to conceal the upper offset of the footings and graded out from the walls and Portico for the width of 20 feet, with a gradual descent down the present surface of the ground. ____________________

Bricks and Mortar. — The whole of the brickwork throughout the building shall be of the best quality of Country or Plantation made bricks, they must be hard and well burnt and laid in mortar composed of the best quality both of fresh Thomaston lime and coarse sharp gritted sand. —— —— The mortar for the foundations, or for all brickwork below the surface of the ground can be made with fresh and well burnt Western lime and Mississippi River or Bayou sand, properly mixed and manipulated as the Superintendent may direct. ——

Slates and Cement. — There shall be two courses of the brickwork laid in fresh hydraulic cement mortar, and a course of strong new Welch slates laid in cement between them, round all the walls and brickwork at the height of 12 inches above the upper offsets of the footings to prevent the ascent of moisture. —— The two upper courses of brickwork of all walls and pediments exposed to the weather shall be laid in the same kind of cement mortar with a course of strong new slates built in between them. The brickwork of the columns shall be built with cement mortar. ——

Footings under Walls. — The footings under all the outside walls shall be in width equal to the length of seven bricks at the bottom; those under the outside walls of the vaults shall be one brick wider; — those under the columns of the Portico shall be Ten bricks square at the bottom; those under the other walls of the Vaults shall be Five bricks wide at the bottom; and those under the 13 in.

Bricks and Mortar. —— The whole of the brickwork throughout the building shall be of the best quality of Country or Plantation made bricks, they must be hard and well burnt and laid in mortar composed of the best quality both of fresh Thomaston lime and coarse sharp gritted sand. ____________

________ The mortar for the foundations or for all brickwork below the surface of the ground can be made with fresh and well burnt Western lime and Mississippi River or Bayou Sand, properly mixed and manipulated as the Superintendent may direct. ____________

Slates and Cement. —— There shall be two courses of the brickwork laid in fresh hydraulic cement mortar and a course of strong new Welch slates laid in cement between them, round all the walls and brickwork at the height of 12 inches above the upper offsets of the footings to prevent the ascent of moisture. __________The two upper courses of brickwork of all walls and pediments exposed to the weather shall be laid in the same kind of cement mortar with a course of strong new slates built in between them. The brickwork of the columns shall be built with cement mortar. ____________

Footings under Walls. —— The footings under all the outside walls shall be in width equal to the length of seven bricks at the bottom; those under the outside walls of the vaults shall be one brick wider; those under the columns of the Portico shall be Ten bricks square at the bottom; those under the other walls of the vaults shall be Five bricks wide at the bottom; and those under the 13 in.

3d

partition walls shall be Four bricks wide at the bottom. After the trenches are properly prepared, the footings shall be laid according to the foregoing mentioned widths, every course of the brickwork (after the first one) shall be diminished in width, by regular offsets of 2¼ inches on each side in the usual manner. ———

Walls. —— The whole of the walls with their base courses, projections, pilasters, cornices, blockings, pediments, arches and other brickwork throughout shall be executed in proper bond, and erected in the most careful, solid and substantial workmanlike manner, according to the forms, heights, and thicknesses shown by and figured on the several drawings herein before referred to.—

Vaults. —— The brickwork of the vaults shall be in accordance with the drawings; the floors to be of bricks laid in cement mortar on brick arches and nine inch dwarf walls; the top of each floor to be plastered with cement mortar floated and finished in a proper manner. The upper arches forming the ceilings shall be two and a half bricks thick; the butments or side walls shall be well tied with wrought iron tie bolts as shown on the Sectional drawing. ———

Arches. —— Foundation walls and strong arches shall be built under the flag-stone floor of the Portico, also under the rear entrance and steps. All the circular headed doorways and windows shall have 9 inch brick arches built through the entire -

partition walls shall be Four bricks wide at the bottom. After the trenches are properly prepared, the footings shall be laid according to the foregoing mentioned widths, every course of the brickwork (after the first one) shall be diminished in width, by regular offsets of 2 ¼ inches on each side in the usual manner. ____________________

Walls. ———— The whole of the walls with their base courses, projections, pilasters, cornices, blockings, pediments, arches, and other brickwork throughout shall be executed in proper bond, and erected in the most careful, solid and substantial workman-like manner, according to the forms, heights, and thicknesses shown by and figured on the several drawings herein before referred to. __________

Vaults. ———— The brickwork of the vaults shall be in accordance with the drawings; the floors to be of bricks laid in cement mortar on brick arches and nine inch dwarf walls; the top of each floor to be plastered with cement mortar floated and finished in a proper manner. The upper arches forming the ceilings shall be two and a half bricks thick; the butments or side walls shall be well tied with wrought iron tie bolts as shown on the Sectional drawing. ____________________________

Arches. ———— Foundation walls and strong arches shall be built under the flag-stone floor of the Portico, also under the rear entrance and steps. All the circular headed doorways and windows shall have 9 inch brick arches built through the entire thickness of the walls; the square headed windows shall have one a half brick splayed arches 4 inches thick on the outside built on 2½ × 5/8 inch iron bars, and 9 inch brick discharging arches turned over wood lintels on the inside. Segmental brick arches one a half brick thick shall be built over the cast iron soffit plates of the front Portico. ———

——— The doorways in the interior partition walls shall have 9 inch segmental arches turned over wood lintels. ———

Columns and other Brickwork. ——— The columns of the Portico shall be carefully built of bricks and cement mortar to the form and dimensions required by the drawings; the bases to be formed in brickwork set on dressed and tooled Northern flagstone plinths 4 inches thick. The capitals to be formed in brickwork; the Abacus to be supported on a strong Northern flag stone—

Cornices &c. ——— The brick cornices throughout shall have their projections supported on a core of strong Northern flag-stones which shall run through the whole thickness of the walls. The brickwork of the entablature and pediment of the Portico shall be supported on Cast iron soffit plates as specified in Iron work. The outside architrave of the three front doorways shall be formed in brick and cement work. ———

— The front and rear Steps shall be well supported on a sufficient number of 9 inch dwarf walls.

Chimneys. — The chimneys to be built with fireplaces where shown on the plans, and with proper size smoke flues well parged on the inside from bottom to top; the hearths thickness of the walls; the square headed windows shall have one a half brick splayed arches 4 inches thick on the outside built on 2½ x ⅝ inch iron bars; and 9 inch brick discharging arches turned over wood lintels on the inside. Segmental brick arches one a half brick thick shall be built over the cast iron soffit plates of the front Portico. ________________ The doorways in the interior partition walls shall have 9 inch segmental arches turned over wood lintels. ________________

Columns and other Brickwork. —— The columns of the portico shall be carefully built of bricks and cement mortar to the form and dimensions required by the drawings; the bases to be formed in brickwork set on dressed and tooled Northern flag-stone plinths 4 inches thick. The capitals to be formed in brickwork, the abacus to be supported in a strong Northern flag stone _____

Cornices etc. —— The brick cornices throughout shall have their projections supported on a core of strong Northern flag-stones which shall run through the whole thickness of the walls. The brickwork of the entablature and pediment of the Portico shall be supported on cast iron soffit plates as specified in Iron work. The outside architraves of the three front doorways shall be formed in brick and cement work. ________________

The front and rear steps shall be well supported on a sufficient number of 9 inch dwarf walls.

Chimneys. —— The chimneys to be built with fireplaces where shown on the plans, and with proper size smoke flues well parged on the inside from bottom to top; the hearths to be of 1¼ inch Welsh slates 15 inches wide laid on 4 inch brick trimmer arches; —

Buttresses. — The buttresses of the front and rear steps shall be built with 9 inch brick walls; the top of each buttress shall be covered with one dressed and tooled Northern flag stone with square and dressed edges. —

Rusticated Work. — The chamfered rusticated work on the outside of the building shall be neatly formed in the brickwork. —

Rear Pediment. — The rear of the building shall have an entablature and pediment similar to the front Portico. —

Stone Masons' Work

Granite Steps. — The front and rear steps leading up to the Portico and rear entrance shall be of best Quincy granite accurately cut, dressed, set and cleaned off, and all joints neatly pointed; that part of the upper step where it comes in front of the columns shall be set before the brickwork of the columns is commenced. —

— The three front doorways to have in each, a granite sill 7 feet 4 inches long by 18 inches wide and 6 inches thick. —

Window Sills. — The whole of the windows, and the two Niches shall have appropriate granite Sills properly cut, dressed and set, and throated underneath. —

to be 1¼ inch. Welsh Slates 15 inches wide laid on 4 inch brick trimmer arches. ________________

Buttresses. —— The buttresses of the front and rear steps shall be built with 9 inch brick walls: the top of each buttress shall be covered with one dressed and tooled Northern flag stone with square and dressed edges. ________________________________

Rusticated Work. —— The chamfered rusticated work on the outside of the building shall be neatly formed in the brickwork. ____________________________

Rear Pediment. —— The rear of the building shall have an entablature and pediment similar to the front Portico. ______

Stone Masons' Work

Granite Steps. —— The front and rear steps leading up to the Portico and rear entrance shall be of best Quincy granite accurately cut, dressed, set and cleaned off, and all joints neatly pointed; that part of the upper step where it comes in front of the columns shall be set before the brickwork of the columns is commenced. ___________ The three front doorways to have in each, a granite sill of 7 feet 4 inches long by 18 inches wide and 6 inches thick. ______________

Window Sills. —— The whole of the windows, and the two Niches shall have appropriate granite Sills, properly cut, dressed, and set, and throated underneath. _______

96

Flagging. — The Portico and Rear entrance landing shall be flagged with best quality hammered, dressed, and tooled Northern flag-stones laid in, and well bedded in good sharp sand mortar; the joints to be made regular, close and even, and the edges round the Portico shall be made square and neatly dressed. ——— ——— Each Vault doorway shall have a dressed and tooled Northern flag-stone sill 3½ feet long and 2 feet 2 inches wide. — Each of the front and rear brick buttresses shall be covered with one large Northern dressed and tooled flag-stone. ——— ——— The plinths under the front Columns shall be 4 inches thick of Northern dressed and tooled flag-stones. ——— ——— The main brick cornices shall be supported on a core of rough Northern flag-stones which shall run through the whole thickness of the walls. — The abacus over the capitals of the columns shall be supported on the same kind of flag-stones. The inside sills for the windows of the vaults shall be of flag-stones well fitted to the outside granite sills. ———

Blacksmith & Founders' Work.

Iron Work for Vaults. ——— The doorway of each Vault shall have a pair of doors on the inside, and a single door on the outside; the inside doors to be made of No. 10 sheet iron rivetted on 1½ × ½ inch wrought iron frame work and well hung to 2½ × ½ inch wrought iron frames, and secured with strong iron bolts and padlock. — The outside door to be made of ⅜ inch Boiler iron rivetted on 2 × ½ inch iron frame work, and

Flagging. ——— The Portico and Rear entrance landing shall be flagged with best quality hammered, dressed, and tooled Northern flag-stones laid in, and well bedded in good sharp sand mortar; the joints to be made regular, close and even, and the edges round the Portico shall be made square and neatly dressed. ____________ Each vault doorway shall have a dressed and tooled Northern flag-stone sill 3 ½ feet long and 2 feet 2 inches wide. ____________ Each of the front and rear brick buttresses shall be covered with one large Northern dressed and tooled flag-stone. ____________ The plinths under the front columns shall be 4 inches thick of Northern dressed and tooled flag-stones. ____________ The main brick cornices shall be supported on a core of rough Northern flag-stones which shall run through the whole thickness of the walls. ____________ The abacus over the capital of the columns shall be supported on the same kind of flag-stones. The inside sills for the windows of the vaults shall be of flag-stones well fitted to the outside granite sills. ____________

Blacksmith and Founders' Work

Iron Work for Vaults. ——— The doorway of each vault shall have a pair of doors on the inside, and a single door on the outside; the inside doors to be made of No. 10 sheet iron riveted on 1½ x ½ inch wrought iron frame work, and well hung to 2½ x ½ inch wrought iron frames, and secured with strong iron bolts and padlock.____ The outside door to be made of ⅛ inch Boiler iron riveted on 2 x ½ inch iron frame work, and

7

hung to a 3 × 5/8 inch wrought iron frame and well secured with a first rate American Bank vault door lock. ——————

—————— The windows in the Vaults shall have in each, a pair of wrought iron sashes, and a pair of wrought iron Shutters; the sashes to be made with 1¼ × ¾ inch outside iron frames filled in with 3/16 × 5/8 inch iron ribs and bars and well hung to 1½ × ½ inch wrought iron frames and secured with strong iron bolts. —

— The shutters to be made with No. 10 sheet iron rivetted on 1½ × ½ inch iron frame work and well hung to 2 × ½ inch wrought iron frames and secured with strong bolts and swivel bar. The whole of the wrought iron frames shall be secured into the brickwork with a sufficient number of iron anchors. —

—————— The arch forming the ceiling of each vault shall have its butments secured with two tie bolts of 2 inch round Tennessee wrought iron with screws and nutts at the ends and cast iron plates 2 feet long by 12 inches wide and 1½ inch thick with flanges cast on the back and built into the brickwork as shown on the drawings. ——————

Iron Work for Roof. —— The two principals for the roof will require the following number of bolts and Straps; Two suspension bolts about 8 feet long made of 1½ inch round Tennessee iron. ——————

Eight bolts about 2 feet long of 1¼ inch square Tennessee iron to secure the Queen posts and principal rafters to the Tie beams. ——————

—— Four Straps of 2½ feet long made of 2½ × ½ inch Tennessee iron to clasp 8 inch timber and provided with suitable bolts about 10 inches long. ——————

— The bolts shall have strong heads and screw ends with suitable Nutts and Washers. ——

hung to 3 x ⅝ wrought iron frame and well secured with a first rate American Bank Vault door lock. ________________ The windows in the vaults shall have in each, a pair of wrought iron sashes and a pair of wrought iron Shutters; the sashes to be made with 1¼ x ¾ inch outside iron frames filled in with ³⁄₁₆ x ⅝ inch iron ribs and bars and well hung to 1½ x ½ inch wrought iron frames and secured with strong iron bolts. ____________ The shutters to be made with No. 10 sheet iron riveted on 1½ x ½ inch iron frame work and well hung to 2 x ½ inch wrought iron frames and secured with strong bolts and swivel bar. The whole of the wrought iron frames shall be secured into the brickwork with a sufficient number of iron anchors. ________________ The arch forming the ceiling of each vault shall have its butments secured with two tie bolts of 2 inch round Tennessee wrought iron with screws and nuts at the ends and cast iron plates 2 feet long by 12 inches wide and 1½ inch thick with flanges cast on the back and built into the brickwork as shown on the drawings. ________________

Iron Work ——— for Roof.

The two principals for the roof will require the following number of bolts and straps: Two suspension bolts about 8 feet long made of 1½ inch round Tennessee iron. ________________ Eight bolts about 2 feet long of 1¼ inch square Tennessee iron to secure the Queen posts and principal rafters to the Tie beams. ________________ Four straps of 2 ½ feet long made of 2 ½ x ½ inch Tennessee iron to clasp 8 inch timber and provided with suitable bolts about 10 inches long. ________________ The bolts shall have strong heads and screw ends with suitable nuts and washers. ________________

8

Wrought Iron Anchors. — A sufficient number of suitable anchors made of 2 × ½ inch Tennessee wrought iron caulked down one inch at the ends and well spiked to the joists and roof timbers, shall be provided to secure the timbers and brickwork together, as shown on the drawings. ———

Arch Bars for Windows. ——— The windows will require the following number of 2½ × ⅝ inch Tennessee wrought iron arch bars. Five bars 5 feet long, — Eight bars 4 feet long; and one bar 7 feet long. ——— ———

Iron Bolts for Trussed Partition. ——— The trussed partition between the Lobby and Court Room will require one suspension bolt 8½ feet long made of 1¼ inch Tennessee wrought iron; and two foot bolts 18 inches long of one inch square iron with heads, screw ends, nutts and washers complete. ———

Iron Ventilators. — Ten appropriate cast iron ventilators 12 × 18 inches in the clear with a 3 inch border shall be provided and set in the base walls where shown on the elevations. ——— ——— The Dome shall have Eight cast iron window guards 3 feet long and 18 inches wide of an appropriate and ornamental pattern made to answer for ventilators. —

Observe. — The Court Room ceiling shall have an ornamental iron ventilator 5 ft. in diameter

Cast iron Lintel Plates. — The brickwork of the front entablature and Pediment of the Portico shall be supported on cast iron lintel plates, cast of proper lengths, 3 feet wide by 1⅜ inch thick with Segmental flanges 15 inches high and ½ inch thick made thus

side view

end view

— The rear entrance shall have one similar lintel — plate 11 feet long and 2½ feet wide. — ——— The front plates to be bolted together in a proper manner; the end plates to be well anchored to the brickwork of the front wall. ———

Wrought Iron Anchors. ——A sufficient number of suitable anchors made of 2 x ½ inch Tennessee wrought iron caulked down one inch at the ends and well spiked to the joists and roof timbers, shall be provided to secure the timbers and brickwork together as shown on the drawings. ____________________

Arch Bars for Windows. ——— The windows will require the following number of 2½ x ⅝ inch Tennessee wrought iron arch bars. Five bars 5 feet long. _______ Eight bars 4 feet long; and one bar 7 feet long. ____________

Iron Bolts for Trussed Partition. ——— The trussed partition between the Lobby and Court Room will require one suspension bolt 8½ feet long made of 1¼ inch Tennessee wrought iron, and two foot bolts 18 inches long of one inch square iron with heads, screw ends, nutts and washers complete. ________________________

Iron Ventilators. ——— Ten appropriate cast iron ventilators 12 x 18 inches in the clear with a 3 inch border shall be provided and set in the base walls where shown on the elevations. _______ The Dome shall have eight cast iron window guards 3 feet long and 18 inches wide of an appropriate and ornamental pattern made to answer for ventilators. ________________

{Observe –The Court Room ceiling shall have ornamental iron ventilator 5 ft. in diameter.}

Cast Iron Lintel Plates. —— The brickwork of the front entablature and pediment of the Portico shall be supported on cast iron lintel plates, cast of proper lengths, 2 feet wide by 1⅜ inch thick with Segmental flanges 15 inches high and 1½ inch thick made thus. _____ The rear entrance shall have one similar lintel _____ plate 11 feet long and 2½ feet wide. _____ [side view sketch and end view sketch] _____ The front plates to be bolted together in a proper manner; the end plates to be well anchored to the brickwork of the front wall. ________________

9

Lightning Rod. —— The building shall be protected from lightning by one of Spratts superior Rods, in ten feet lengths, with accurately fitted brass screw connecting joints, also glass isolaters &c. complete, fixed on the top of the Dome on an ornamental wrought iron Standard, and carried from thence down to the ground, and mounted with one of Waddelles improved points,

Dock Railing &c. — The dock in the court room shall have iron gates and railing 5 feet high, made with 7/8 inch round iron, with spear heads 4 inches apart. ——

Coppersmiths' Work

Roof Gutters. Pipes &c. —— The gutters on each side of the roof shall be made 30 inches wide with sheets of the best quality of 12 lb. Braziers copper properly lapped, grooved and soldered and turned up against the walls under 12 lb. copper flashings 7½ inches wide lapped 2 inches over one another at the ends and built 3½ inches into the brickwork; there shall be two copper eave pipes about 5 feet long and 8 inches square on each side of the building, built in the brickwork as shown on the Transverse section, ——— The inclined valley gutters shall be 24 inches wide of 12 lb. copper sheets, lapped and grooved, and the edges laid on proper cant strips. Each side of the building shall have two rain water pipes from the eave pipes down to the ground made of ×× tin 5 inches in diameter, the same to have plain moulded heads at the top and appropriate cast iron Guard boxes at the bottom. — — The pediment walls above the roof and the chimney tops shall have proper copper flashings. The scuttle frame and cover shall be lined with Copper. —

Lightning Rod. —— The building shall be protected from lightning by one of Spratt's superior Rods, in ten feet lengths, with accurately fitted brass screw connecting joints, also glass isolaters etc. complete, fixed on the top of the Dome on an ornamental wrought iron standard, and carried from thence down to the ground, and mounted with one of Waddell's improved points.

Dock Railing etc. —— The dock in the court room shall have iron gates and railing 5 feet high, made with ⅞ inch round iron, with spear heads 4 inches apart. ________

Coppersmiths' Work

Roof Gutters —— Pipes etc.

The gutters on each side of the roof shall be made 30 inches wide with sheets of the best quality of 12 lb. Braziers copper properly lapped, grooved and soldered and turned up against the walls under 12 lb. copper flashings 7½ inches wide lapped 2 inches over one another at the ends and built 3½ inches into the brickwork; there shall be two copper eave pipes about 5 feet long and 8 inches square on each side of the building, built in the brickwork as shown on the Transverse section. ________ The inclined valley gutters shall be 24 inches wide of 12 lb. copper sheets, lapped and grooved, and the edges laid on proper cant strips. Each side of the building shall have two rain water pipes from the eave pipes down to the ground made of xx tin 5 inches in diameter, the same to have plain moulded heads at the top and appropriate cast iron Guard braces at the bottom. ________ The pediment walls above the roof and the chimney tops shall have proper copper flashings. The scuttle frame and cover shall be lined with copper.

10

Covering Cupulo. —— The Cupulo 6½ feet high as shown from A to B on the flank elevation, with the projection of the cornice shall be covered with best quality 12 lb. Braziers Copper sheets - properly lapped and grooved, and put on in the neatest and best workmanlike manner.

The top of the octagonial lantern above the cupulo shall be covered inlike manner.

Slaters' Work.

Slating. —— The roof shall be sheathed with Gang sawyed inch Yellow Pine or Cypress sheathing boards and slated with the best quality of 10 × 20 inch Welch Slates put on with five inches lap or cover and properly bonded, especially at the eaves and heading courses, and warranted perfectly tight and free from leaks for One Year after the building is finished.

The ridges and hips shall be covered with good English ridge tiles laid in and pointed with white sharp sand Mortar. — All the slating is to be rendered up perfect on the completion of the building. ——

Carpenters' & Joiners' Work.

Timbers & Plank. —— All the timbers and plank used in the erection of the building shall be of the best description of the sound Yellow Pine or Cypress, proper for the uses for which it is designed, free from unsound Knots, splits or rot. ——

Covering Cupulo. —— The cupulo 6½ feet high as shown from A to B on the flank elevation, with the projection of the cornice shall be covered with best quality 12 lb. Braziers copper sheets properly lapped and grooved, and put on in the neatest and best workmanlike manner. The top of the octagonal lantern above the cupulo shall be covered in like manner.

Slaters' Work

Slating. ———— The roof shall be sheathed with Gang sawyed inch Yellow Pine or Cypress sheathing boards and slated with the best quality of 10 x 20 inch Welch Slates put on with five inches lap or cover and properly bonded, especially at the eaves and heading courses, and warranted perfectly tight and free from leaks for One Year after the building is finished.

The ridges and hips shall be covered with good English ridge tiles laid in and painted with white sharp sand mortar. ____________ All the slating is to be rendered up perfect on the completion of the building. ________________

Carpenters' and Joiners' Work

Timbers and Plank. — All the timbers and plank used in the erection of the building shall be of the best description of the sound Yellow Pine or Cypress, proper for the uses for which it is designed, free from unsound knots, splits or rot. _______________

Lumber. — The Joiners' work to be of clear and well seasoned best quality Cypress or white pine (except otherwise mentioned) free from saps, Knots, shakes or other defects. —

Dimensions of Timbers. Framing &c. — The floor joists shall be 3 × 12 inches; those for the 1st floor to be 20 inches from centres, and those for the 2nd floor 16 inches; each floor to have one row of 1½ × 4 inch × bridging pieces; Trimmers and trimmer joists to be 4 × 12 inches; Ceiling joists for the Jury Rooms and Lobby shall be 3 × 8 in; those for Court Room 2 × 8 inches all placed 16 inches from centres. The wood partitions to be made of 6 × 6 inch posts and braces, 4 × 6 inch plates, and 3 × 6 inch studding placed 18 inches from centres. The sides of each partition shall be diagonally furred with 2 × 1 inch laths 12 inches from centres. — — The partition between the Lobby and Court Room shall be framed and trussed according to the sectional drawing. —

— The ceiling of the Court Room shall be diagonally furred similar to the sides of the partitions. —

Roof and Dome. — The Roof and Dome shall be framed and constructed in the most skilful and best workmanlike manner with timbers according to the dimensions figured on the drawings; — The roof to have two framed principals as per transverse section, also trussed purlins over the wood partitions, and upright stanchions where necessary. —

— The ceiling of the Portico shall be formed into three panels with wood framed work prepared to receive lath and plastering.

Lumber. ——— The Joiners' work to be of clear and well seasoned best quality Cypress or white pine (except otherwise mentioned) free from sap, knots, shakes or other defects. ________________

Dimensions of Timbers Framing etc. —— The floor joists shall be 3 x 12 inches; those for the 1st floor to be 20 inches from centres and those for the 2nd floor 16 inches; each floor to have one row of 1½ x 4 inch x bridging pieces. Trimmers and trimmer joists to be 4 x 12 inches, Ceiling joists for the Jury Rooms and Lobby shall be 3 x 8 in., those for the Court Room 2 x 8 inches all placed 16 inches from centres. The wood partitions to be made of 6 x 6 inch posts and braces, 4 x 6 inch plates, and 3 x 6 inch studding placed 18 inches from centres. The sides of each partition shall be diagonally furred with 2 x 1 inch laths 12 inches from centres. ________ The partition between the Lobby and Court Room shall be framed and trussed according to the sectional drawing. ____________ The ceiling of the Court Room shall be diagonally furred similar to the sides of the partitions. ________

Roof and Dome. ——— The Roof and Dome shall be framed and constructed in the most skilful and best workmanlike manner with timbers according to the dimensions figured on the drawings: ________ the roof to have two framed principals as per transverse section, also trussed purlins over the wood partitions, and upright Stanchions where necessary. __________ The ceiling of the Portico shall be formed into three panels with wood framed work prepared to receive lath and plastering.

12

Sheathing Roof. — The plain of the roofing shall be sheathed with Gang sawyed one inch Yellow Pine or Cypress boards. —

Scuttle. — The roof shall have a scuttle 2½ feet long and 20 inches wide in the clear, with a wood frame and cover lined with copper; the cover to be hung with suitable hinges and fastened on the inside with an iron hook & eye. — The Lobby ceiling shall have a scuttle of the same size finished with dressed and beaded casings and with dressed wood cover properly hung with hinges; from this scuttle to the one in the roof there shall be fixed over the ceiling joists a rough gang-way of inch boards.

Bond and Anchor Timbers. — Bond and Anchor timbers of proper dimensions shall be provided and built into the brickwork where the Superintendent may direct. —

Other Timbers. — All other timbers not herein particularly mentioned, and which may be found necessary to complete the building shall be of proper dimensions and furnished in sufficient quantities. —

Floors. — All the floors throughout the interior of the building (except those for the Vaults) shall be laid with best quality Mill-dressed Yellow Pine planks not over 5½ inches wide and 1¼ inch thick perfectly well seasoned put down in straight courses with tongued and grooved edges secret nailed. — ~~The~~ joints to be neatly smoothed off. — The floors over the ceiling of the Vaults shall be laid on 2×4 inch Yellow Pine Sleepers 18 inches from centres. —

Sheathing Roof. —— The plain of the roofing shall be sheathed with Gang Sawyed one inch Yellow Pine or Cypress boards. ____

Scuttle. —— The roof shall have a scuttle 2½ feet long and 20 inches wide in the clear, with a wood frame and cover lined with copper: the cover to be hung with suitable hinges and fastened on the inside with an iron hook and eye. ____
The Lobby ceiling shall have a scuttle of the same size finished with dressed and beaded casings and with dressed wood cover properly hung with hinges, from this scuttle to the one in the roof there shall be fixed over the ceiling joists a rough gang-way of inch boards.

Bond and Anchor Timbers. —— Bond and Anchor timbers of proper dimensions shall be provided and built into the brickwork where the Superintendent may direct. ____

Other Timbers. —— All other timbers not herein particularly mentioned, and which may be found necessary to complete the building shall be of proper dimensions and furnished in sufficient quantities. ____

Floors. —— All the floors throughout the interior of the building (except those for the vaults) shall be laid with best quality mill-dressed Yellow Pine planks not over 5½ inches wide and 1¼ inch thick perfectly well seasoned put down in straight courses with tongued and grooved edges secret nailed. ____ the joints to be neatly smoothed off. ____ The floors over the ceiling of the vaults shall be laid on 2 x 4 inch Yellow Pine Sleepers 18 inches from centres. ____

13

Finish of Dome. — The Dome shall be sided up with 1¼ inch milldressed Yellow pine planks not over 3½ inches wide and perfectly well seasoned, and put together with white lead in the joints; the base, cornice and mouldings to be neatly finished according to the drawings. The openings to be finished with dressed casings, and with 1¾ inch Louvre blinds, put inside the iron window guards so as to make them perfectly water tight. — The Cupola to be properly sheathed to receive the Copper covering. The whole of the wood finishings shall be properly painted and sanded, and made perfectly water tight.

Wainscotting. — The walls and partitions round the Court Room shall be wainscotted 3½ feet high from the floor with narrow matched and beaded dressed 1¼ inch Yellow Pine planks finished with moulded cappings and skirtings. —

Skirtings. — All the apartments throughout (except the vaults) shall have skirtings with a single faced plinth 10 inches deep capped with a 3 inch base moulding. Turned knobs of wood shall be fixed into the skirtings behind each door to prevent the lock handle from breaking the plastering. —

Stairs. — The stairs shall be made with 2 inch good clear heart Yellow Pine treads and 1¼ inch Cypress risers finished with moulded

Finish of Dome. ——— The Dome shall be sided up with 1¼ inch milldressed Yellow Pine planks not over 3½ inches wide and perfectly well seasoned, and put together with white lead in the joints; the base, cornice and mouldings to be neatly finished according to the drawings. The openings to be finished with dressed casings, and with 1¾ inch Louvre blinds, put inside the iron window guards so as to make them perfectly water tight. ________________ The Cupulo to be properly sheathed to receive the Copper covering. The whole of the wood finishings shall be properly painted and sanded and made perfectly water tight.

Wainscotting. ——— The walls and partitions round the Court Room shall be wainscotted 3½ feet high from the floor with narrow matched and beaded dressed 1¼ inch Yellow Pine planks finished with moulded cappings and skirtings. ____________________

Skirtings. ——— All the apartments throughout (except the vaults) shall have skirtings with a single faced plinth 10 inches deep capped with a 3 inch base moulding. Turned knobs of wood shall be fixed into the skirtings behind each door to prevent the lock handle from breaking the plastering. ______________

Stairs. ——— The stairs shall be made with 2 inch good clear heart Yellow Pine treads and 1¼ inch Cypress risers finished with moulded

14)

and returned nosings and mounted on strong timber carriages and beaded string boards. — the landing to have dressed and beaded facias The ends of the steps to be housed into — moulded wall boards. —— The handrail to be of Oak, finished 4½ inches wide and 3½ inches thick ~~and~~ handsomely moulded, and mounted on fancy turned Cypress balusters 3 inches in diameter grained in imitation of oak. The newells to be of Cypress, fancy turned, 10 inches in diameter finished with a moulded Oak cap to correspond with the handrail. ——

Doorways. —— The three front doorways shall have 4×14 inch solid timber frames with wood reveal casings on the outside to receive the cement architraves, and 10 inch heavy band moulded architraves on the inside, the frames to have imposts and glazed headlights, each doorway shall have a pair of 2¼ inch heavy and full moulded paneled doors as per drawings well hung with best butts and secured with the best description of top and bottom wrought iron bolts, The centre doorway and the one leading into the Sheriff's office shall have the best Kind of American Store door locks. All the other doorways (except those leading from the Lobby into the Court Room) shall have 1¾ inch full moulded paneled doors well hung with 4½ × 4½ inch best butts and fastened with first rate American 8 inch Rim locks with Pearl white Knobs. All doorways to be trimmed on the inside with 10 inch heavy-band moulded architraves with plinth blocks;-

and returned nosings and mounted on strong timber carriages and beaded string boards. The landing to have dressed and beaded facias. The ends of the steps to be housed into moulded wall boards. ______________________ The handrail to be of Oak finished 4½ inches wide and 3¼ inches thick handsomely moulded, and mounted on fancy turned Cypress balusters 3 inches in diameter grained in imitation of oak. The newell to be of Cypress, fancy turned, 10 inches in diameter finished with a moulded Oak cap to correspond with the handrail.______________________

Doorways. ————— The three front doorways shall have 4 x 14 inch solid timber frames with wood reveal casings on the outside to receive the cement architraves, and 10 inch heavy band moulded architraves on the inside, the frames to have imposts and glazed headlights; each doorway shall have a pair of 2¼ inch heavy and full moulded paneled doors as per drawings well hung with best butts and secured with the best description of top and bottom wrought iron bolts. The centre doorway and the one leading into the Sheriff's office shall have the best kind of American Store door locks. All the other doorways (except those leading from the Lobby into the Court Room) shall have 1¾ inch full moulded paneled doors well hung with 4½ x 4½ inch best butts and fastened with first rate American 8 inch Rim locks with Pearl white Knobs. All doorways to be trimmed on the inside with 10 inch heavy-band moulded architraves with plinth blocks;

15

those in the brick walls to have 2 inch moulded paneled jambs and heads; those in the wood partitions to have 2 inch plain rebated jambs,

The Rear entrance doorway to have side and headlights; the side lights to have 1 3/8 inch paneled shutters properly hung and fastened,

——— The doorways leading from the Lobby into the Court Room shall have in each, a pair of 1 1/2 inch Fly doors, with light panels covered with green baize, hung with 4×4 inch butt hinges, and furnished with Knobs, springs &c. complete. The two fold doors shall have wrought iron bolts. ———

Windows.— The whole of the windows (except those in the Vaults) shall be finished with plain jambs; 10 inch band moulded architraves, and with moulded paneled backs; each window to have a pair of 1 3/4 inch glazed sashes double hung in boxed and cased frames with patent axle pullies, (extra size) iron sash weights and best patent Sash cords; The frames shall be made with 1 1/2 inch pulley styles, 1 1/8 inch inside and outside casings, two inch sub sills and heads; inside and outside stops and beads to be 1 1/2 inches by 5/8 of an inch.—

The outside of the frames shall have a wood bead 1 1/2 in. in diameter. The window in the Sheriff's Office and those in the Clerk of the Court and Recorder's Offices shall have 1 3/8 inch four fold mortice blind shutters made in two heights, hung with best butts and flaps and secured on the inside of each office with iron swivel bars, bolts &c. complete— and furnished with shutter Knobs, The sashes of the same windows shall have Mackerall's brass sash fasteners fixed on the meeting rails.—

those in the brick walls to have 2 inch moulded paneled jambs and heads; those in the wood partitions to have 2 inch plain rebated jambs. The Rear entrance doorway to have side and headlights, the side lights to have 1⅜ inch paneled shutters properly hung and fastened. ________ The doorways leading from the Lobby into the Court Room shall have in each, a pair of 1½ inch Fly doors, with light panels covered with green baize, hung with 4 x 4 inch butt hinges, and furnished with knobs, springs etc. complete. The two fold doors shall have wrought iron bolts. __________

Windows. ______

The whole of the windows (except those in the vaults) shall be finished with plain jambs; 10 inch band moulded architraves, and with moulded paneled backs, each window to have a pair of 1¾ inch glazed sashes double hung in boxed and cased frames with patent axle, pullies, (extra size) iron sash weights and best patent sash cord; The frames shall be made with 1½ inch pulley styles, 1⅛ inch inside and outside casings, two inch sub sills and heads; inside and outside stops and beads to be 1½ inches by ⅝ of an inch. _____ The outside of the frames shall have a wood bead 1½ in. in diameter. The window in the Sheriff's office, and those in the Clerk of the Court and Recorder's Offices shall have 1⅜ inch four fold mortice blind shutters—made in two heights, hung with best butts and flaps and secured on the inside of each office with iron swivel bars, bolts etc. complete—and furnished with shutter knobs; the sashes of the same windows shall have Mackerall's brass sash fasteners fixed on the meeting rails.

16

Wood Mantels. —— The fireplaces throughout the building (except those in the vaults) shall have appropriate pilaster wood mantels of a bold pattern set on Slate hearths and painted in imitation of marble; each fireplace including those in the vaults shall have a large iron grate with ash pan, fender and appurtenances complete of the value of Fifteen dollars when set and finished. ——

Finish of Court Room. —— The Court Room must be fitted, with its railings 4½ × 3 inches, moulded, and fancy turned newells 6 inches diameter, and fancy-turned balusters 2½ inches diameter all of Cypress grained in imitation of Oak. The Judge's seat, desk, &c. the Clerk's seat and desk, the seats for the Spectators, witnesses, and Jury and all other fittings shall be made and finished in the very best workmanlike manner. ——

—— The Clerk and Judges desks must be made of a good quality of mahogany; all other fittings to be of Cypress or white Pine. ——

—— The Dock to have a wrought iron railing about 5 feet high with iron doors &c. Complete. — The large Archway shall be finished with plastered jambs and Soffit and with 14 inch large band moulded double faced architraves executed in plaster work; the angles to have wood beads; the plinths at bottom shall be executed in wood work. ——

—— The judge's seat or stand must be raised three risers of eight inches, the clerks one riser of eight inches, and the jury, witnesses & spectators seats must rise three inches, at least, to each seat, as the retire from the bar. ——

Wood Mantels. ——

The fireplaces throughout the building (except those in the vaults) shall have appropriate pilaster wood mantels of a bold pattern set on slate hearths and painted in imitation of marble; each fireplace including those in the vaults shall have a large iron grate with ash pan, fender and appurtenances complete of the value of Fifteen dollars when set and finished. ____________

Finish of Court Room. ——

The Court Room must be fitted, with its railings 4½ x 3 inches, moulded, and fancy turned newells 6 inches diameter, and fancy—turned balusters 2½ inches diameter all of Cypress grained in imitation of Oak. The Judge's seat, desk, etc. the Clerks, seat and desk, the seats for the Spectator's witnesses, and Jury and all other fittings shall be made and finished in the very best workmanlike manner. ______ The Clerk and Judges desk's must be made of a good quality of mahogany; all other fittings to be of Cypress or White Pine. ______ The Dock to have a wrought iron railing about 5 feet high with iron doors etc. Complete. ______ The large Archway shall be finished with plastered jambs and soffit and with 14 inch large band moulded double faced architraves executed in plaster work; the angles to have wood beads; the plinths at bottom shall be executed in wood work. ______ The judge's seat or stand must be raised three risers of eight inches, the clerks one riser of eight inches, and the jury, witnesses and spectator's seats must rise three inches, at least, to each seat, as the retire from the bar. ______

17

Plasterers' Work

Outside Plastering. — The outside surface of the brickwork allround the building including the top of the parapets and Pediments, and chimney tops, buttresses, and Columns shall be plastered in the very best manner with cement mortar composed of the best quality of fresh hydraulic cement and coarse sharp gritted washed sand, properly mixed and put on in the most judicious and careful manner, colored and jointed to imitate light brown stone Masonry. — — The chamfered rusticated work, main cornice, mouldings, belt courses &c. shall be executed in a proper manner. The shafts of the columns shall be fluted according to the Order of architecture; the bases and capitals to be finished in cement work. The panels in the front and sides of the building shall have large mouldings. The panels of the Portico ceiling shall be lathed and plastered, and finished with mouldings corresponding with the outside architrave moulding. The ceiling of the rear entrance shall be finished in like manner.

Inside Plastering. — All the ceilings and wood partitions must be lathed, and plastered in three coats hardfinished; All the walls must be plastered with two coats, and left coarse finished with the float, and properly whitened. The vaults to be plastered and whitened in a proper manner and finished with a cement base 12 inches high; their floors shall be plastered with cement. The Court Room to have a plaster cornice at the angles of the ceiling, worth 60 cts. per running foot; all other apartment to be left plain,

Plasterers' Work

Outside Plastering. —— The outside surface of the brickwork allround the building including the top of the parapets and Pediments, and chimney tops, buttresses, and columns shall be plastered in the very best manner with cement mortar composed of the best quality of fresh hydraulic cement and coarse sharp gritted washed sand, properly mixed and put on in the most judicious and careful manner, colored and jointed to imitate light brown stone Masonry. ______ The chamfered rusticated work, main cornice, mouldings, belt courses etc. shall be executed in a proper manner. The shafts of the columns shall be fluted according to the Order of architecture, the bases and capitals to be finished in cement work. The panels in the front and sides of the building shall have large mouldings. The panels of the Portico ceiling shall be lathed and plastered, and finished with mouldings corresponding with the outside architrave moulding. The ceiling of the rear entrance shall be finished inlike manner.

Inside Plastering. —— All the ceilings and wood partitions must be lathed, and plastered in three coats hardfinished; All the walls must be plastered with two coats, and left coarse finished with the float, and properly whitened. The vaults to be plastered and whitened in a proper manner and finished with a cement base 12 inches high; their floors shall be plastered with cement. The Court Room to have a plaster cornice at the angles of the ceiling, worth 60 cts. per running foot; all other apartments to be left plain.

16 18

Painters' and Glaziers' Work

Painting.—— All the wood and iron work usually painted of the inside and outside of the building shall have four good coats of pure white lead and pure linseed oil, mixed with such plain colors as may be chosen. All the inside wood work to be finished flat. The fittings, railings, seats, &c. in the Court Room, and all the wooden doors throughout the building, as well as the newels and balusters of the stairway shall be grained in imitation of Oak and well varnished. The oak rail to be varnished and polished. — ———— The wood and Copper work of the Dome shall be well painted and sanded. — The Seven wood mantels shall be finished in imitation of Egyptian Marble and varnished; The tin rain water pipes to be properly painted.

Glazing.—— All the glazing must be done with the best quality of Single thickness French window glass, well bedded back, puttied, and left clean and perfect on the completion of the building. —— The number of lights, sizes, &c. to be as indicated on the drawings. ————

General Conditions.—— All the work is to be done in the best and most workmanlike manner, of proper and appropriate materials, according to the elevations, plans and sections herein before cited and the foregoing specifications; and every thing necessary to the proper and complete execution of said plans is to be done and finished whether

Painters' and Glaziers' Work

Painting. —— All the wood and iron work usually painted of the inside and outside of the building shall have four good coats of pure white lead and pure linseed oil mixed with such plain colors as may be chosen. All the inside wood work to be finished flat. The fittings, railings, seats, etc. in the Court Room, and all the wooden doors throughout the building, as well as the newell and balusters of the stairway shall be grained in imitation of Oak and well varnished. The oak rail to be varnished and polished. ______ The wood and copper work of the Dome shall be well painted and sanded. ______ The Seven wood mantels shall be finished in imitation of Egyptian marble and varnished: The tin rain water pipes to be properly painted.

Glazing. ———— All the glazing must be done with the best quality of Single thickness French window glass, well bedded back, puttied, and left clean and perfect on the completion of the building. ______ The number of lights, sizes, etc., to be as indicated on the drawings.

General Conditions. —— All the work is to be done in the best and most workmanlike manner, of proper and appropriate materials, according to the elevations, plans and sections herein before cited and the foregoing specifications; and everything necessary to the proper and complete execution of said plans is to be done and finished whether

19

the same may have been herein specified or not.

And all such necessary work and materials which may not have been set forth in this specification, is to be done and are to be furnished in a manner corresponding with the rest of the work, as faithfully and as well as though the same were herein particularly described and provided for. —————— Every part of the building is to be executed under the Superintendance of [redacted], and to be subject to their entire approval, and in case any omissions, alterations or additions of the plans may be required during the progress of the work, the same shall be carried into effect, without in any way violating or vitiating any Contract which may have been made for work or materials; and all such omissions, additions or alterations shall be estimated for, and the value thereof agreed upon and approved by the Superintendents, and added to or deducted from the contract, as the case may be, by an endorsement on the same before going into execution, or no allowance will be made for them by either party. ——————

—— The building shall be completely finished and delivered up to the building Committee on or before the first day of March in the year 1861, on failure whereof the Contractor shall forfeit and pay to the said Committee the sum of Five dollars for every day the building remains unfinished after that time, which sum the Committee shall be allowed to stop out of any moneys that may be due and owing to the Contractors on account of the works.

—— During the progress of the works, payments shall be made (as may be hereafter agreed upon between the Committee and Contractor) only on the written certificate of the Superintendents. ——————

Over

the same may have been herein specified or not. And all such necessary work and materials which may not have been set forth in this specification, is to be done and are to be furnished in a manner corresponding with the rest of the work, as faithfully and as well as though the same were herein particularly described and provided for. ______ Every part of the building is to be executed under the superintendence of [text redacted], and to be subject to their entire approval, and in case any omissions, alterations or additions of the plans may be required during the progress of the work, the same shall be carried into effect, without in any way violating or vitiating any contract which may have been made for work or materials; and all such omissions, additions or alterations shall be estimated for, and the value thereof agreed upon and approved by the Superintendents, and added to or deducted from the contract, as the case may be, by an endorsement on the same before going into execution, or no allowance will be made for them by either party. ______ The building shall be completely finished and delivered up to the building committee on or before the first day of March in the year 1861, on failure whereof the Contractor shall forfeit and pay to the said Committee the sum of Five dollars for every day the building remains unfinished after that time; which sum the Committee shall be allowed to stop out of any moneys that may be due and owing to the contractors on account of the works. ______ During the progress of the works, payments shall be made (as may be hereafter agreed upon between the Committee and Contractor) only on the written certificate of the Superintendents. ____________

over

The Contract was made and signed on the thirtieth day of November Eighteen hundred Fifty Nine

Witness—

F. H. Legendre
L. E. Lanoux

M. Springer
S. S. Evans
J. J. Thompson
P. H. Gary
F. L. Blanchard
W. L. Gaudi
C. Lazarde

The contract was made and signed on the thirteenth day of November Eighteen hundred fifty nine

Witnesses

F. H. Legendre
L. E. Lamoreux

M. Springer
S. S. Evans
J. F. Thompson
P. H. Gary
O. L. Blanchard
Chs. F. Gaudet
C. Lagarde

Bibliography

Primary Sources

Manuscript Collections

Cemetery Listings, St. John's Episcopal Church Library, Thibodaux, LA.

Dinsmore, James. Journal from Natchez, May 1824–1827. MS 1016, Dinsmore Family Papers. Dinsmore Farm Library, Dinsmore Homestead Foundation, Burlington, KY. https://www.dinsmorefarm.org/library/letters-journals-poetry/.

Historical Research Center of the Diocese of Houma/Thibodaux, Thibodaux, LA.

Lafourche American Revolution Bicentennial Commission and Lafourche Heritage '76 Collection, MS-00029. Nicholls State University Archives and Special Collections, Thibodaux, LA.

Lafourche Parish Courthouse Records, MS-00188. Nicholls State University Archives and Special Collections, Thibodaux, LA.

Maude H. Billiu Collection, MS-00020. Nicholls State University Archives and Special Collections, Thibodaux, LA.

Menard, Charles M. *Annals of the Church of St. Joseph,* 1842, 1844, 1845. Charles M. Menard Collection, MS-00166. Nicholls State University Archives and Special Collections, Thibodaux, LA.

St. Matthews Episcopal Church Records, MS 000207. St. John's Episcopal Church, Thibodaux, LA.

William Littlejohn Martin Collection, MS-00011. Nicholls State University Archives and Special Collections, Thibodaux, LA.

Maps

Map Display, Digital/Sanborn Maps, 1867–1920. Nicholls State University Archives and Special Collections, Thibodaux, LA.

Plan of the Thibodaux Saw Mill Co. property by St. Mary St., March 4, 1869. J. A. and J. C. Lovell Collection, MS-00085. Nicholls State University Archives and Special Collections, Thibodaux, LA.

Poussin, Guillaume Tell. *1817 Reconnoitering Chart of the South Frontier of the United States of America from the River Perdido Towards the East as Far as the River Sabine to the West.* Office of the Chief of Engineers, Record Group 77. National Archives Records Administration, Washington, DC.

Newspapers

Assumption Pioneer (Napoleonville, LA)

Bayou Catholic (Schriever, LA)

Genius of Liberty, and Fayette Advertiser (Uniontown, PA)

Hartford Courant (CT)

Intelligencer, and Lafourche and Terrebonne Advertiser (Thibodaux, LA)

Lafourche Comet (Thibodaux, LA)

New Orleans Crescent

New Orleans Democrat

New Orleans Times-Picayune

St. Charles Herald (Hahnville, LA)

San Antonio Daily Light (TX)

Thibodaux Minerva (LA)

The Weekly Thibodaux Sentinel (LA)

Government Documents: State, County, Parish

Louisiana

Assumption Parish Miscellaneous Records, No. 13.

Lafourche Parish Civil Suits, Second Judicial District Court.

Lafourche Parish Civil Suits, Fifth Judicial District Court.

Lafourche Parish Marriage Records.

Lafourche Parish Miscellaneous Records, Books 1, 2.

Lafourche Parish Police Jury Laws and Ordinances No. 1.

Lafourche Parish Police Jury Record D, 1852–1862.

Lafourche Parish Records, Conveyances.

Lafourche Parish Records, Official Acts.

Lafourche Parish Records, Original Acts.

Lafourche Parish Succession/Probate Records.

Louisiana State Legislature, Acts Passed by the 1830 Session.

Terrebonne Parish Records, Conveyances.

Terrebonne Parish Records, Original Acts.

Thibodaux Town Council Records, Book 1, 1838–1862.

Georgia

Morgan County Records, Deed Book C.

Government Documents: United States

1850 United States Federal Census.

1860 United States Federal Census.

1870 United States Federal Census.

1880 United States Federal Census.

Hahn, Thurston H. G. III, *Historical and Archaeological Investigations at the Wetlands Acadian Cultural Center, Thibodaux, Louisiana.* Coastal Environments, Inc., 1992.

The War of the Rebellion: A Compilation of the Official Records of the Union and Confederate Armies. 70 volumes in 4 series. Washington, DC: Government Printing Office, 1880–1901. Republication, Harrisburg, PA: National Historical Society, 1971. Reprint, Historical Times, 1985.

Published Correspondence, Memoirs, Diaries, and Other Materials

Burnham, Roderick H. *The Burnham Family, or Genealogical Records of the Four Emigrants of the Name, Who Were among the Early Settlers of America*. Hartford, CT: Press of Case, Lockwood, & Brainard, 1869. www.familysearch.org/library/books/idviewer/374161.

Champomier, P. A. *Statement of the Sugar Crop Made in Louisiana in 1845–1846*. (New Orleans: n.p., 1846). https://archive.org/details/ldpd_6413611_000.

Duncan, Herman Cope. *The Diocese of Louisiana, Some of Its History, 1838–1888: Also some of the History of Its Parishes and Missions, 1805–1888*. New Orleans: A. W. Hyatt, 1888.

Ellis, Franklin, ed. *History of Fayette County, Pennsylvania, with Biographical Sketches of Many of Its Pioneers and Prominent Men*. Philadelphia: L. H. Everts & Co., 1882. https://digital.library.pitt.edu/islandora/object/pitt%3A00aft2784m/viewer.

Gardner, Charles, comp. *Gardner's New Orleans Directory for 1861, Including Jefferson City, Gretna, Carrollton, Algiers, and McDonough, with a New Map of the City, Street and Levee Guide, Business Directory, An Appendix of much Useful Information, and a Planter's Directory, Containing the Names of Cotton and Sugar Planters of Louisiana, Mississippi, Arkansas, and Texas*. New Orleans: Charles Gardner, 1861. https://www.civilwarphilatelicsociety.org/wp-content/uploads/2019/06/Res-Arch-Dir-New-Orleans-Dir-1861.pdf.

Grisamore, S. T. "Fifty Years Ago." Lafourche Parish Louisiana, Genealogy Trails History Group. Transcribed and submitted by Savanna. Accessed October 22, 2025. https://genealogytrails.com/lou/lafourche/his_50yearsago.html.

Lafever, Minard. *The Modern Builder's Guide*. New York: Dover Publications, 1969. Reprint of 1833 Edition.

Unpublished Correspondence and Interviews

Ann Parkerson Burke, telephone interviews with David Plater, various dates.

Clifton Theriot, email correspondence with David D. Plater, various dates.

DeeDee Dibenedetto, email correspondence with David D. Plater, various dates.

Jo D. Norton, email correspondence with David D. Plater, various dates.

Jo D. Norton email to Judith Soniat, Genealogy Department, Terrebonne Parish Library, February 12, 2018.

Laura Browning, email correspondence with David D. Plater, June 7–8, 2019.

Marshall Woody Williams, copy of correspondence with Jo D. Norton, November 18, 2009.

Richard Bourgeois, telephone interview with David D. Plater, September 28, 2025.

Private Collections

Jo D. Norton, New Iberia, Louisiana.

David D. Plater, Thibodaux, Louisiana.

Secondary Sources

Books

Blackburn, Florence, and Fay G. Brown, eds. *Franklin Through the Years.* Florence Blackburn and Fay G. Brown, 1972.

Brantley, Robert S., with Victor McGee. *Henry Howard, Louisiana's Architect.* The Historic New Orleans Collection and Princeton Architectural Press, 2015.

Brown, Jefferson Beale. *Key West: The Old and the New.* The Record Company, 1912.

Casey, Powell A. *Encyclopedia of Forts, Posts, Named Camps, and Other Military Installations in Louisiana, 1700–1981.* Claitor's Publishing Division, 1983.

Cenac, Christopher, Sr., and Claire Domangue Joller. *Hard Scrabble to Hallelujah: Legacies of Terrebonne Parish, Louisiana.* Vol. I, *Bayou Terrebonne.* JFC, LLC, 2016.

Chauvin, Phillip, Jr. *The Weekly Thibodaux Sentinel Microfilm Index August 5, 1865—December 7, 1912.* Terrebonne Genealogical Society, 1996.

Chauvin, Philip, Jr., and Phoebe Chauvin Morrison. *1880 U.S. Census, Lafourche Parish, Louisiana.* Terrebonne Genealogical Society, Inc., 1999.

Conrad, Glenn R., ed. *New Iberia: Essays on the Town and Its People,* 2nd ed. Center for Louisiana Studies, University of Southwestern Louisiana, 1986.

Dudley, Tara A. *Building Antebellum New Orleans: Free People of Color and Their Influence.* University of Texas Press, 2021.

Follett, Richard. *The Sugar Masters: Planters and Slaves in Louisiana's Cane World, 1820–1860.* Louisiana State University Press, 2005.

Hébert, Donald J. *South Louisiana Records: Church and Civil Records of Lafourche-Terrebonne Parishes.* Vol. 1, 1794–1840. Donald Hébert, 1978.

Hébert, Donald J. *South Louisiana Records: Church and Civil Records of Lafourche-Terrebonne Parishes.* Vol. 2, 1841–1850. Donald J. Hébert, 1978.

Hébert, Donald J. *South Louisiana Records: Church and Civil Records of Lafourche-Terrebonne Parishes.* Vol. 3, 1851–1860. Donald J. Hébert, 1979.

Hébert, Donald J. *South Louisiana Records: Church and Civil Records of Lafourche-Terrebonne Parishes.* Vol. 4, 1861–1870. Donald J. Hébert, 1979.

Kramer, Thomas Frere. *A Family Montage: Being the Families Kramer, Frère, Foster, Marsh, Gates, and Allied Families.* Center for Louisiana Studies, University of Louisiana at Lafayette, 2002.

Martin, William Littlejohn. *Records and Recollections of Thibodaux, Louisiana.* Compiled by Philip Uzee. Thibodaux: Woman's Club of Thibodaux, Louisiana, 1972.

Morrison, Phoebe Chauvin, annot. *Re-Annotated 1860 Census of Terrebonne Parish, Louisiana. June 4, 1860.* Terrebonne Genealogical Society, 1992.

Morrison, Phoebe Chauvin, annot. *1870 U.S. Census, Terrebonne Parish, LA (Annotated).* Terrebonne Genealogical Society, 2002.

Morrison, Phoebe Chauvin, comp. *1860 Census, Lafourche Parish, LA.* Terrebonne Genealogical Society, 2001.

Newton, Milton B., Jr. *Louisiana House Types: A Field Guide.* Mélanges, no. 2. Museum of Geoscience, Louisiana State University, 1971.

Plater, David D., ed. *"The Remarkably Neat Church in the Village of Thibodaux": An Antebellum History of St. John's Episcopal Church.* St. John's Episcopal Church and the Center for Louisiana Studies, 1994. Reprint, Copy Connection, 2016.

Sloan, Eric. *A Museum of Early American Tools.* Ballantine Books, 1974.

Smith, J. Frazer. *White Pillars: Early Life and Architecture of the Lower Mississippi Valley Country.* Bramhall House, 1941.

Terrebonne Genealogical Society. *1870 U.S. Census, Lafourche Parish, LA.* Terrebonne Genealogical Society, Inc., 2002.

Terrebonne Genealogical Society. *1870 U.S. Census, Terrebonne Parish, LA (Annotated).* Terrebonne Genealogical Society, 2002.

Terrebonne Genealogical Society. *Terrebonne Life Lines* 9, no. 4 (Winter 1990).

Terrebonne Genealogical Society. *Terrebonne Life Lines* 18, no. 4 (Winter 1999).

Terrebonne Genealogical Society. *Terrebonne Life Lines* 19, no. 2 (Summer 2000).

Terrebonne Genealogical Society. *Terrebonne Parish 1880 United States Census.* Terrebonne Genealogical Society, 1999.

Terrebonne Genealogical Society Census Committee. *The Terrebonne Parish 1860 Census, June 4, 1860.* Terrebonne Genealogical Society, 1983.

Thompson, V. Elaine. *Clinton, Louisiana: Society, Politics, and Race Relations in a Nineteenth-Century Southern Small Town.* University of Louisiana at Lafayette Press, 2014.

Tocqueville, Alexis de. *Democracy in America.* Translated by Harvey C. Mansfield and Delba Winthrop. The University Press of Chicago, 2002.

Toups, Kenneth B., and June B. Foret. *1860 Census, Lafourche Parish, LA.* Toups Enterprises, 1986.

Uzee, Philip D. *Thibodaux Chronicles: A Sesquicentennial History*. Portier Gorman Publications, 1987.

Vlach, John Michael. *Back of the Big House: The Architecture of Plantation Slavery*. University of North Carolina Press, 1993.

Westerman, Audrey B., copier and indexer. *Lafourche Parish, Louisiana, Census 1850*. Nicholls State University Library, 1979.

Articles and Websites

1842 New Orleans City Directory. USGenWeb Archives. Accessed September 3, 2020. http://files.usgwarchives.net/la/orleans/history/directory/1842ad-i.txt.

Ancestry. "John Bellsen." Louisiana, U.S. Compiled Marriage Index, 1718–1925. Accessed May 23, 2023. https://www.ancestry.com/search/collections/7837/.

Ancestry. "Sciotha S. Evans." Louisiana, U.S. Compiled Marriage Index, 1718–1925. Accessed June 6, 2023, https://www.ancestry.com/search/collections/7837.

Ancestry. "Message Boards, Ragan Family." Accessed December 5, 2019. https://www.ancestry.com.au/boards/localities.northam.usa.states.louisiana.parishes.lafourche/208.

Ball's Place Blog. "James Frost–Phoebe Greene." Last updated July 11, 2018. http://www.ballsplace.com/HowellsHTML/f213.htm.

"The Benjamin Franklin Holdens: A Story." *St. John's Historic Cemetery Association Newsletter* (February–March 2020). https://www.stjhca.org/visit-1.html.

Brownlee, Henry French, abstractor, and Maggie Stewart, ed. and formatter. "1850 Federal Census, Lafourche Parish, Louisiana." USGenWeb, 2006. http://files.usgwarchives.net/la/lafourche/census/1850/pg287b.txt.

Daigle, Cynthia, submittor. "Cemetery Listings for: St. John's Episcopal Cemetery, Thibodaux, Lafourche Parish, LA." Modified and resubmitted by Chris Tidwell, April 25, 2015. USGenWeb, http://files.usgwarchives.net/la/lafourche/cemeteries/stjohnepiscopal.txt.

Docufree Cemetery Find. "Sarah F. Burnham." Accessed May 15, 2023. https://cemeteryfind.com.

Fayette County Historical Society. "Tragic Springer House Fire." *The Fayette Gazette* (First Quarter, 2016).

Find a Grave. "Capt Edward Truman Burnham." Accessed August 6, 2023. www.findagrave.com/memorial/76015621/edward-truman-burnham.

Find a Grave. "Ellen Maria Burnham Biddle." Accessed May 16, 2023. https://www.findagrave.com/memorial/27479931/ellen-maria-biddle.

Find a Grave. "James Aaron Frost Sr." Accessed December 4, 2025. https://www.findagrave.com/memorial/23443845/james-aaron-frost.

Find a Grave. "John Bellsen." Accessed August 2, 2023. www.findagrave.com/memorial/22923549/john-bellsen.

Find a Grave. "Katherine Collins 'Kate' Burnham Stebbins." Accessed September 9, 2022. https://www.findagrave.com/memorial/27480153/katherine-collins-birmingham.

Find a Grave. "Lelia 'Lee' Bellsen McCoy." Accessed August 2, 2023. www.findagrave.com/memorial/66171773/lelia-mccoy.

Find a Grave. "Louisa Delphine Burnham Birmingham." Accessed September 9, 2022. https://www.findagrave.com/memorial/27479938/louisa-delphine-birmingham.

Find a Grave. "Mary J. Evans." Accessed August 11, 2023. https://www.findagrave.com/memorial/23452177/mary-j-evans.

Find a Grave. "Morgan Springer (1814–1861)." Accessed July 24, 2015. https://www.findagrave.com/memorial/23510810/morgan-springer.

Find a Grave. "Sarah Elizabeth Barbre Bellsen." Accessed May 23, 2023. www.findagrave.com/memorial/22923566.

Find a Grave. "Sciotha S. Evans." Accessed August 2, 2023. www.findagrave.com/memorial/60330347/sciotha-s-evans.

Gaubert, Denis. "A Story, Part II: The Rev. Charles Felix Dixon Lyne." *St. John's Historic Cemetery Association Newsletter* (Fall 2023). https://www.stjhca.org/visit-1.html.

Genealogy.com. "William Gaddis—Frederick Co VA 1740s." Accessed July 13, 2018. https://www.genealogy.com/forum/surnames/topics/gaddis/1003/.

Kniffen, Fred B. "Louisiana House Types." *Annals of the Association of American Geographers* 26, no. 4 (December 1936): 179–92.

Lowery, Charles. "The Great Migration to the Mississippi Territory, 1798–1819." Mississippi History Now, November 2000. https://www.mshistorynow.mdah.ms.gov/issue/the-great-migration-to-the-mississippi-territory-1798-1819.

"Minutes of Police Jury of Terrebonne." *Terrebonne Life Lines* 18, no. 2 (1999): 127.

Morgan, Stuart. "A Belief in the Power of Concealed Shoes: Investigating the Age-Old Superstition of Hiding Footwear Within the Structure of a Building.'" *Satra Bulletin* (May 2018): 50. https://www.Satra.com/bulletin/article.php?id=2078.

MyHeritage. "Almira Frost: Historical Records and Family Trees." Accessed April 22, 2019. www.myheritage.com/names/almira_frost.

"Record of Marriages 1858–1882." *Terrebonne Life Lines* 21, no. 4 (Winter 2002).

RootsWeb's World Connect Community Trees Index. "Authement, Patchett, Savoie, Daigle Connection." Accessed April 22, 2019. http://wc.rootsweb.ancestry.com/cgi-bin/igm.cgi?db=cynthiadaigle [website no longer active, as of December 17, 2025].

RootsWeb's World Connect Community Trees Index. "My Father's Ancestors and Their Descendants 10 July 2015." Accessed August 25, 2015. http://rootsweb.ancestry.com/cgibin/igm.cgi?op=GET&db=m-faatdo61515&id=I14358 [website no longer active, as of December 17, 2025].

Route40.net. "Levi Springer House." Accessed June 20, 2018. http://www.route40.net/page.asp?n=10847.

Ruth, Philip, and Kenneth J. Basalik. "The Searight Tavern: Fixture Along the National Road." *Seeking Searights and Shaws: Archaeological Investigations of Two National Road Era Sites in Fayette County,*

Pennsylvania. Cultural Heritage Research Services, Inc., 2008. http://chrsinc.com/wp-content/themes/chrs/pdfs/seeking_searights.pdf.

"Shubael Tenney: A Story." *St. John's Historic Cemetery Association Newsletter* (February–March 2018). https://www.stjhca.org/visit-1.html.

"TGS Newsletter," *Terrebonne Life Lines* 22, no. 12 (March 2003).

USGenWeb Archives. "Center Cemetery, East Hartford, Hartford County, Connecticut." Accessed October 16, 2020. http://files.usgwarchives.net/ct/hartford/cemeteries/cen-a-c.txt.

Webster, Ian. "Value of 1837 Dollars Today Inflation Calculator." CPI Inflation Calculator. Accessed February 4, 2023. https://www.official-data.org/US/inflation/1837.

Wikipedia. "Josiah Frost House." Accessed July 10, 2018. https://en.wikipedia.org/wiki/Josiah_Frost_House.

Wikipedia. "National Register of Historic Places listings in Fayette County, Pennsylvania." Accessed September 17, 2025, https://en.wikipedia.org/wiki/National_Register_of_Historic_Places_listings_in_Fayette_County,_Pennsylvania.

Wikipedia. "Wallace-Baily Tavern." Accessed October 7, 2019. https://en.wikipedia.org/wiki/Wallace-Baily_Tavern.

WikiTree. "Aaron Grinage (abt. 1778)." Accessed December 1, 2025. http://wikitree.com/wiki/Grinage-65.

WikiTree. "James Grinage (1801)." Accessed December 1, 2025. https://www.wikitree.com/wiki/Grinage-66.

WikiTree. "John Kees (1763–1807)." Accessed July 20, 2023. https://WikiTree.com/wiki/Kees-39.

WikiTree. "Levi Springer Jr. (1777–1862)." Accessed July 13, 2018. https://www.wikitree.com/wiki/Springer-588.

WikiTree. "Levi Springer Sr. (1744–1823)." Accessed June 10, 2018. https://www.wikitree.com/wiki/Springer-64.

WikiTree. "Sumner Towsend (abt. 1805–1881)." Accessed July 31, 2023. www.wikitree.com/wiki/Townsend-53.

WikiTree. "Zadock Springer (1770–1844)." Accessed June 10, 2018. https://www.wikitree.com/wiki/Springer-1892.

Zemba, Liz. "Loss of Historic Fayette Farmhouse Blamed on Vandals." *Trib Live* (Tarentum, PA), April 28, 2015. https://archive.triblive.com/news/loss-of-historic-fayette-farmhouse-blamed-on-vandals/.

Theses and Dissertations

Collopy, Catherine T. "Seeking the Middle in a Sectionalizing America: James Dinsmore and the Shaping of Regional Economies, 1816–1872." PhD diss., University of Cincinnati, 2015.

Poetry

Whitman, Walt. "I Hear America Singing." In *Leaves of Grass* (New York: W.E. Chapin & Co., Printers, 1867).

Endnotes

Preface

1. Florence Blackburn and Fay G. Brown, eds., *Franklin Through the Years* (Florence Blackburn and Fay G. Brown, 1972); Glenn R. Conrad, ed., *New Iberia: Essays on the Town and Its People*, 2nd ed. (Center for Louisiana Studies, University of Southwestern Louisiana, 1986); Thomas Frere Kramer, *A Family Montage: Being the Families Kramer, Frere, Foster, Marsh, Gates, and Allied Families* (Center for Louisiana Studies, University of Louisiana at Lafayette, 2002); Christopher E. Cenac Sr. and Claire Domangue Joller, *Hard Scrabble to Hallelujah: Legacies of Terrebonne Parish, Louisiana: Legacies of Terrebonne Parish, Louisiana,* vol. 1, *Bayou Terrebonne* (JPC, LLC, 2016).

2. S. T. Grisamore, "Fifty Years Ago," trans. and submitted by Savanna, Lafourche Parish Louisiana, Genealogy Trails History Group, accessed October 27, 2025, https://genealogytrails.com/lou/lafourche/his_50yearsago.html; William Littlejohn Martin, *Records and Recollections of Thibodaux, Louisiana,* comp., Philip D. Uzee (The Woman's Club of Thibodaux, Louisiana, 1972); David D. Plater, ed., "*The Remarkably Neat Church in the Village of Thibodaux": An Antebellum History of St. John's Episcopal Church* (St. John's Episcopal Church and Center for Louisiana Studies, 1994; with reprint edition by Copy Connection, 2016); Philip D. Uzee, *Thibodaux Chronicles: A Sesquicentennial History* (Portier Gorman Publication, 1987).

3. For the architect Henry Howard and his influence in the Lafourche region, see Robert S. Brantley, with Victor McGee, *Henry Howard, Louisiana's Architect* (The Historic New Orleans Collection and Princeton Architectural Press, 2015). On southeast Louisiana's "Bluff Country" see V. Elaine Thompson, *Clinton, Louisiana: Society, Politics, and Race Relations in a Nineteenth-Century Southern Small Town* (University of Louisiana at Lafayette Press, 2014). For a recent work on the building trade involving free people of color in antebellum New Orleans, see Tara A. Dudley, *Building Antebellum New Orleans: Free People of Color and Their Influence* (University of Texas Press, 2021).

4. See Grisamore, "Fifty Years Ago."

Chapter One

1. A representation of the narrow, cleared areas of Bayou Lafourche and the Mississippi River banks is seen in the map of Guillaume Tell Poussin, *1817 Reconnoitering Chart of the Southern Frontier of the United States of America from the River Perdido Towards the East as Far as the River Sabine to the West* (File No.

58–1/2 Fortification Papers 1815–1818 Letters Received), Office of the Chief of Engineers, Record Group 77, National Archives, Washington, DC.

2. For the geology and the pre- and early European settlement of Bayou Lafourche and Bayou Terrebonne, see Thurston H. G. Hahn, III, *Historical and Archaeological Investigation of the Wetlands Acadian Cultural Center, Thibodaux, Louisiana* (Coastal Environments, Inc., 1992), chapter 2.

3. See Milton B. Newton Jr., *Louisiana House Types: A Field Guide*, Mélanges, no. 2 (Museum of Geoscience, Louisiana State University, 1971), 13–15. Newton used Fred B. Kniffen, "Louisiana House Types," in *Annals of the Association of American Geographers* 26, no. 4 (December 1936), provided courtesy Dr. Richard Campanella, Tulane University.

4. For more on early-nineteenth-century Bayou Lafourche, see Col. William W. Pugh, "Bayou Lafourche from 1820 to 1825: Its Inhabitants, Customs, and Pursuits," from *The Louisiana Planter and Sugar Manufacturer*, MS-00011, Loc. B, Box 4, Item 21, William Littlejohn Martin Collection, Nicholls State University Archives; Col. William W. Pugh, "Reminiscences of an Old Fogey," beginning June 6, 1881, in *The Pioneer of Assumption Parish*, MS-00011, William Littlejohn Martin Collection, Nicholls State University Archives.

5. For Bayou Teche, see Backburn and Brown, eds., *Franklin through the Years*, 14, 15–18; Dr. Alfred Duperie, "A Narrative of Events Connected with Early Settlement of New Iberia," 73–113, and Carl A. Brasseaux, "New Iberia's Steamboat Days," 264–275, in Conrad, ed., *New Iberia*. An alternate, significant small-craft trade route from the Lafourche region was via the Attakapas Canal, from Napoleonville on Bayou Lafourche to Lake Verret and the Atchafalaya Basin, and on west to Bayou Teche.

6. The arpent, a French unit of measure equal to about 192 English feet, remained in use in Louisiana throughout the twentieth century alongside the "acre" measure of approximately 208.71 feet, brought to the region by Americans.

7. Lafourche Parish, LA, Records, Original Acts 1813, fol. 101 (March 20, 1813); Lafourche Parish, LA, Records, Conveyance Book (COB) A, fol. 363 (1818) [Lafourche conveyance books will be designated by the term COB and appropriate letters or numbers.]; Pugh, "Reminiscences of an Old Fogey," June 18, 1881; Blackburn and Brown, eds., *Franklin through the Years*, 9.

8. Soon after purchasing the tract between Jackson and Maronge Streets, H. S. Thibodaux contracted with Benjamin Winchester to sell him the eight-arpent parcel. Winchester was to assume the debt represented by unpaid notes between Malbrough and Henry Johnson, but the obligation was taken over by Thibodaux in the acquisition of the 5¾-arpent parcel from Johnson. Likely because of a default by Winchester, the sale to Winchester did not consummate. Thibodaux remained owner of the eight arpents fronting Bayou Lafourche. Lafourche Parish, LA, Records, COB A, fol. 364 (June 8, 1822).

Chapter Two

1. "Aaron Grinage (abt. 1778)," WikiTree, accessed December 1, 2025, http://wikitree.com/wiki/Grinage-65.

2. "James Grinage (1801)," WikiTree, accessed December 1, 2025, https://www.wikitree.com/wiki/Grinage-66; see also Donald Hébert, *South Louisiana Records: Church and Civil Records of Lafourche-Terrebonne Parishes.* Vol.1, 1794–1840. (Donald Hébert, 1978), 241; Sale to Grinage, Lafourche Parish, LA, Records COB D, fol. 437 (April 16, 1828).

3. "James Grinage (1801)," WikiTree.

4. Lafourche Parish, LA, Records, COB H, 147 (August 5, 1830).

5. Acts passed by the Session of the Legislature of the State of Louisiana, 1830, 126.

6. Martin, *Records and Recollections,* 8–9, 16, 34; Minutes, Thibodaux Town Council Records, Book 1, June 18 and 24, 1838, and March 31, 1841; Grisamore, "Fifty Years Ago," October 25, 1890.

7. Martin, *Records and Recollections*, 16, 34.

8. Martin, *Records and Recollections*, 16.

9. Newton, *Louisiana House Types*, 13–15; *The Weekly Thibodaux Sentinel*, August 22, 1874, p. 1.; Pugh, "Reminiscences of an Old Fogey," July 16, 1881.

10. Book 1, Thibodaux Council Minutes, June 18 and 24, 1838.

11. Blackburn and Brown, eds., *Franklin through the Years*, 14, 15–18; Duperie, "A Narrative of Events," and Brasseaux, "New Iberia's Steamboat Days," 110–111, 262–269; Pugh, "Reminiscences of an Old Fogey," June 25, 1881.

12. Minutes, Thibodaux Town Council Records, Book 1, March 8 and May 21, 1842.

13. Minutes, Thibodaux Town Council Records, Book 1, April 12, 1843, November 14, 1843, and February 23, 1860.

14. See, e. g., Minutes, Thibodaux Town Council Records, Book 1, April 12, 1842, and May 6, 1848.

15. Minutes, Thibodaux Town Council Records, Book 1, June 18, 1838.

16. William W. Pugh, "Bayou Lafourche from 1820 to 1825," in *The Louisiana Planter and Sugar Manufacturer*, MS-00011, Martin Collection, Nicholls State University Archives.

17. Minutes, Thibodaux Town Council Records, Book 1, September 4, 1838, April 12, 1842, and April 12, 1843.

18. Minutes, Thibodaux Town Council Records, Book 1, August 6, 1838, June 24, 1839, July 15, 1843, July 15, 1846, September 9, 1847, December 19, 1848, and May 4, 1856.

[19] Minutes, Thibodaux Town Council Records, Book 1, September 19, 1840.

[20] Minutes, Thibodaux Town Council Records, Book 1, May 1, 1842.

[21] Thibodaux Ice Company Lease, Lafourche Parish, LA, Records, COB B, fol. 218.

[22] *Thibodaux Minerva*, August 6, 1853, p. 1, www.newspapers.com/image/367154236/.

Chapter Three

[1] Katherine T. Collopy, "Seeking the Middle in a Sectionalizing America: James Dinsmore and the Shaping of Regional Economies, 1816–1872" (PhD diss., University of Cincinnati, 2015), 60 and n. 25.

[2] "John Kees (1763–1807)," WikiTree, accessed July 5, 2023, https://www.wikitree.com/wiki/Kees-39.

[3] Jo Norton to Judith Soniat, Terrebonne Parish, LA, Genealogy Department, February 12, 2018.

[4] Morgan County, Georgia, Deed Book C, 208, 233; "TGS Newsletter," *Terrebonne Life Lines* 22, no. 12 (March 2003); Marshall Woody Williams to Jo D. Norton, November 18, 2009 (copy at Morgan County, Georgia, Archives).

[5] Succession of Absalom Kees, Probate No. 883, Lafourche Parish, LA, Records.

[6] US Federal Census 1860.

[7] On Natchez's growth and importance, see Charles Lowery, "The Great Migration to the Mississippi Territory, 1798–1819," Mississippi History Now, November 2000, https://mshistorynow.mdah.ms.gov/issue/the-great-migration-to-the-mississippi-territory-1798-1819.

[8] James Dinsmore Journal from Natchez, May 1824–1827, MS 1016, Dinsmore Family Papers, Dinsmore Homestead Foundation, Farm Library, Burlington, KY, https://www.dinsmorefarm.org/library/letters-journals-poetry/; Collopy, "Seeking the Middle," 60 and fn. 25; Jo Norton to David Plater, e-mails February 11 and 14, 2018. The US Census in 1830 showed "Key, Absom" in Terrebonne Parish, but no other family members were recorded there. See Rev. Donald Hebert, *South Louisiana Records: Church and Civil Records of Lafourche-Terrebonne Parishes,* Vol. I: 1794–1840 (Rev. Donald Hebert, 1978), 549; and for additional evidence of Kees's continued presence in 1830, a suit was filed that year in Terrebonne against Kees, see *Terrebonne Life Lines* 9, no. 4 (Winter 1990): 20–21.

[9] Lafourche Parish, LA, Records COB I, folios 83 and 190; and COB K, fol. 281. For the Hawley and Larkin lot transactions, see Lafourche Parish Courthouse Records, MS-00188, Accessions 025–004–004 and 011–005–010, Nicholls State University Archives and Special Collections.

[10.] Lafourche Parish, LA, Records, General Index to Conveyances, T-Z, for record of Union Bank mortgages beginning 1833; Lafourche Parish, LA, Records, COB L, fol. 407 (April 28, 1836); Lafourche Parish, LA, Records, COB P, fol. 259 (April 16, 1839).

[11.] MS-00188, Accession 066–004–001, Nicholls State University Archives.

[12.] Lafourche Parish, LA, Records, COB O, folio 253 (March 9, 1838).

[13.] Lafourche Parish, LA, Records, COB P, fol. 382 (April 11, 1839).

[14.] Lafourche Parish, LA, Records, COB R, folio 97 (August 7, 1840), and COB U, folio 53 (April 19, 1844).

[15.] On the Thibodaux Saw Mill and the Foley/Townsend association, see "Town Directory," *Thibodaux Minerva*, November 5, 1853, https://www.loc.gov/item/sn86079110/1853-11-05/ed-1/; "Sumner Townsend (abt. 1805–1881)," Wikitree, accessed July 31, 2023, https://www.wikitree.com/wiki/Townsend-53.

[16.] Lafourche Parish, LA, Records, Succession of A. M. Foley, COB 10, folio 132 (March 21, 1866).

[17.] Lafourche Parish, LA, Records, COB P, fol. 259 (04/15/1839). Comparative US dollars are found in Ian Webster, "Value of 1837 Dollars Today Inflation Calculator," CPI Inflation Calculator, accessed February 4, 2023, https://www.officialdata.org/us/inflation/1837. In March 1842, the Union Bank branch in Thibodaux was robbed, its vault having been broken into from underneath the raised structure. The entire vault contents, $31,000, were stolen. Much of the loot was recovered and the perpetrators were tried and punished. Source: Grisamore, "Fifty Years Ago," June 11, 1892.

[18.] Plater, ed., "*The Remarkably Neat Church,*" 54–57.

[19.] Minutes, Thibodaux Town Council Records, Book 1, May 14, 1839; May 4, 1840; May 4, 1846.

[20.] See, e.g., "Josiah Frost House," Wikipedia, accessed July 10, 2018, https://en.wikipedia.org/wiki/Josiah_Frost_House; and "National Register of Historic Places listings in Fayette County, Pennsylvania," Wikipedia, accessed September 17, 2025, https://en.wikipedia.org/wiki/National_Register_of_Historic_Places_listings_in_Fayette_County,_Pennsylvania.

[21.] Plater, ed., *"The Remarkably Neat Church,"* 10–13, 37, 39–40, 42–62. A recorded act of donation of the Ridgefield Plantation property where St. John's was built never has been located in the Lafourche Parish Records.

[22.] Lafourche Parish, LA, Records, COB P, Folio 259 (April 15, 1839).

[23.] Plater, ed., *"The Remarkably Neat Church,"* 10, 12, 37, 39–40. For short biographies of the church founders, see *"The Remarkably Neat Church," passim*, and for a printed copy of the September 1843 building contract for St. John's, see "*The Remarkably Neat Church,*" Appendix B, 90–92. For an example of 1840 period masonry (brick and sandstone) construction featuring a Greek Revival style portico in Fayette County, Pennsylvania, see "Wallace-Baily Tavern," Wikipedia, accessed July 5, 2023, https://en.wikipedia.org/wiki/Wallace_Baily_Tavern. Federal style sandstone and brick construction were more common than Greek Revival building styles in western Pennsylvania in the early nineteenth century.

Chapter Four

1. Plater, ed., "*The Remarkably Neat Church*," 12, 77n29.

2. Plater, ed., "*The Remarkably Neat Church*," 78n29.

3. *Daily Picayune* (New Orleans, LA), July 20, 1843, p. 3 (courtesy of Robert J. Cangelosi Jr., October 13, 1997).

4. Building Contract, Lafourche Parish, LA, Records, COB T, Fol. 289, September 28, 1843 [copy in Plater, ed., "*The Remarkably Neat Church,*" 11–13, 90, and n29].

5. Minard Lafever, *The Modern Builders Guide* (Dover Publications, Inc., 1969 reprint of 1833 edition), v-vi ff., x. A helpful list of handbooks in use in the time period and a discussion of their utility is in J. Frazer Smith, *White Pillars: Early Life and Architecture in the Lower Mississippi Valley Country* (Bramhall House, 1941), 223. Examples of antebellum American South outbuildings using Greek Revival period design are featured in John Michael Vlach, *Back of the Big House: The Architecture of Plantation Slavery* (University of North Carolina Press, 1993), 92 and 114. In 2019 the owners of the c. 1853 Magnolia Plantation house on LA 311 in Terrebonne Parish donated a Greek Revival-style privy, now restored, to the LSU Rural Life Museum in Baton Rouge.

6. St. John's Building Contract, Lafourche Parish, LA, Records, COB T, Fol. 289 (September 28, 1843).

7. *Terrebonne Life Lines* 9, no. 4 (Winter 1990): 30.

8. The original St. John's slate roof proved defective, requiring replacement in 1856, when the church was renovated. See Building Contract, Lafourche Parish, LA, Records, Miscellaneous Book 2, 175–83.

9. Plater, ed., "*The Remarkably Neat Church,*" 57–58, 90.

10. Lafourche Parish, LA, Records, COB Y, fol. 345 (September 20, 1847); COB Y, fol. 358 (October 7, 1847); and COB Z, fol. 27, (January 10, 1848).

11. MS-00188, Accession 011–005–017 (October 26, 1842); and Lafourche Parish, LA, Records, COB T, Fol. 30 (October 26, 1842), and COB Y, fol. 14 (March 26, 1847).

12. Brantley and McGee, *Henry Howard*, 30.

[13.] Silas Grisamore, *The Weekly Thibodaux Sentinel,* August 22, 1874, p. 1. The description is supplemented in Grisamore, "Fifty Years Ago," December 13, 1890.

[14.] Questions remain about the living conditions and work of skilled and unskilled or domestic enslaved people in bayou-side, rural Louisiana towns like Thibodaux. Recorded references are skimpy, and more research is needed on these topics. The experiences of the state's sugar plantation-based enslaved workers, including the many skilled ones, and the practice of leasing them, are described in Richard Follett, *The Sugar Masters: Planters and Slaves in Louisiana's Cane World, 1820–1860* (Louisiana State University Press, 2005), 80–84, and chapters 3 and 4.

[15.] Plater, ed., *"The Remarkably Neat Church,"* Exhibit B.

[16.] For the lot sale transactions on the east side of Jackson Street, Thibodaux, see Lafourche Parish, LA, Records, COB L, fol. 407 (June 7, 1836); and MS-00188, Accession 024–004–013, Nicholls State University Archives.

[17.] Lafourche Parish, LA, Records, COB U, fol. 153 (June 18, 1844).

[18.] On the Jackson Street, Thibodaux, lot conveyance to the Methodist Episcopal Church, which prohibited "any other purpose or object" on the site, see Lafourche Parish, LA, Records, COB U, fol. 204 (September 5, 1844).

[19.] Lafourche Parish, LA, Records, COB U, fol. 153 (June 18, 1844).

[20.] On the market square job, see the building contract between Brigitte B. Thibodaux and Absalom Kees, see Lafourche Parish, LA, Records, COB U, fol. 4 (June 13, 1845); and for the job fulfillment arrangement with Thibodaux's son Henry C. Thibodaux, see COB U, fol. 4 (June 13, 1846); and COB Y, fol. 73 (September 20, 1847). Several drawings of elevations and floor plans of the structures were created by Kees and were identified as part of the "act of building between A Kees and Mrs H S Thibodaux," dated June 13, 1845, and signed by James McAllister, judge. See MS-00188, Accession 177–003–001, Nicholls State University Archives.

[21.] MS-00188, Accession 77-003-001, Nicholls State University Archives.

[22.] Martin, *Records and Recollections*, 38, 45; "Thibodeaux, Lafourche Parish, Louisiana, June, 1885," Sanborn Map & Publishing Company Limited New York, Map Display: Digital Sanborn Maps, 1867–1970, Nicholls State University Archives.

[23.] *Terrebonne Life Lines* 18, no. 2 (Summer 1999): 127 (Ref. Minutes of Police Jury of Terrebonne Parish, Book A, 1822–1847, fol. 383 [October 5, 1846]).

[24.] For Kees's sale of Nathan and his enslaved artisans between March 1847 and January 1848, see Lafourche Parish, LA, Records COB Y, fol. 14; COB Y, fol. 45; COB Y, fol. 358; COB Z, fol. 27; and *supra*, fn. 39.

[25.] For the will of Rachel Tabor, see MS-00188, Accession 009–001–018, Nicholls State University Archives.

[26] Fifth Judicial District Court Civil Suit, 444 (1849), Lafourche Parish, LA, Records.

[27] Lafourche Parish, LA, Records, Fifth Judicial District Court Civil Suit 705 (1850–1852), and MS-00188, Accession 092–005–009, Nicholls State University Archives.

[28] 1850 United States Federal Census; Audrey B. Westerman, copier and indexer, *Lafourche Parish, Louisiana, Census 1850* (Nicholls State University Library, 1979), 46.

[29] Lafourche Parish, LA, Records, COB Z, fol. 191 (March 30, 1848).

[30] MS-00188, Accession 177–001–001, Nicholls State University Archives.

[31] Lafourche Parish, LA, Records, COB EE, fol. 475 (March 25, 1852).

[32] Lafourche Parish, LA, Records, COB FF, fol. 115 (July 30, 1852); Terrebonne Parish, LA, Records, COB O, fols. 516 & 517 (July 30, 1852, and September 15, 1852).

[33] Lafourche Parish, LA, Records, COB GG, fol. 195 (December 23, 1853), and COB 2, fol. 109 (February 1, 1855).

[34] Advertisement, "A. Kees, Lockport, Dec. 10, 1853," *Thibodaux Minerva*, December 31, 1853.

[35] The various sales from the Sawmill Plantation property, totaling twenty-one and a half arpents frontage on Bayou Lafourche, are found at Lafourche Parish, LA, Records: COB 2, fol. 244; COB 2, fol. 396; COB 2, fol. 485; COB 3, fol. 27; COB 3, fol. 377; COB 3, fol. 378; and COB 3, fol. 590. A probably unrelated, coincidence was the 1860 marriage of Wayne Tanner to Julia F. Burnham, a daughter of master carpenter Edward T. Burnham. The marriage was held by Reverend T. R. B. Trader at St. John's Episcopal Church in Thibodaux on December 11, 1860. "Record of Marriage," *Terrebonne Life Lines* 21, no. 4 (Winter 2002): 292.

[36] 1860 United States Federal Census. Information on George Davis, husband of Mary Kees, is from a telephone conversation with Jo Norton, of New Iberia, LA, a descendant of Mary Kees and George Davis, April 22, 2023. The birth of Robert Meegel was November 11, 1851, recorded at Lockport's Holy Savior Catholic Church as that of Robert Miguel, of parents Eduard Miguel (for Meegel) and Amelia Kise (for Kees). Donald J. Hébert, *South Louisiana Church and Civil Records, Lafourche-Terrebonne Parishes*, vol. 3: 1851–1860 (Donald J. Hébert, 1978), 366.

[37] Lafourche Parish LA Records, COB 9, fols. 225 and 259 (January 8, 1861, and April 11, 1863).

[38] *Democracy in America*. Trans., Harvey C. Mansfield and Delba Winthrop (University of Chicago Press, 2002), 526–29.

Chapter Five

1. "James Frost-Phoebe Greene," Ball's Place Blog, last updated July 11, 2018, http://www.ballsplace.com/HowellsHTML/f213.htm; "James Aaron Frost Sr.," Find a Grave, accessed December 4, 2025, https://www.findagrave.com/memorial/23443845/james-aaron-frost.

2. Philip Ruth and Kenneth J. Basalik, "The Searight Tavern: Fixture Along the National Road," in *Seeking Searights and Shaws: Archaeological Investigations of Two National Road Sites in Fayette County, Pennsylvania* (Cultural Heritage Research Services, Inc., 2008), http://chrsinc.com/wp-content/themes/chrs/pdfs/seeking_searights.pdf; "Josiah Frost House," Wikipedia.

3. "Morgan Springer (1814–1861)," Find a Grave, accessed July 24, 2015, https://www.findagrave.com/memorial/23510810/morgan-springer; "William Gaddis—Frederick Co VA 1740s," Genealogy.com, accessed July 13, 2018, https://www.genealogy.com/forum/surnames/topics/gaddis/1003/.

4. "Levi Springer Sr. (1744–1823)," WikiTree, accessed June 10, 2018, https://www.wikitree.com/wiki/Springer-64; Franklin Ellis, ed., *History of Fayette County, Pennsylvania, with Biographical Sketches of Many of Its Pioneers and Prominent Men* (L. H. Everts & Co., 1882), 699ff; "Levi Springer Jr. (1777–1862)," WikiTree, accessed July 13, 2018, https://www.wikitree.com/wiki/Springer-588.

5. "Zadock Springer (1770–1844)," WikiTree, accessed June 10, 2018, https://www.wikitree.com/wiki/Springer-1892.

6. *The Genius of Liberty, and Fayette Advertiser*, Library of Congress, accessed June 26, 2018, https://lccn.loc.gov/sn85054556.

7. Ellis, *History of Fayette County, Pennsylvania*, 134–35, 672–73.

8. "Levi Springer House," Route 40.net, accessed June 20, 2018, https://www.route40.net/page.asp?n=10847.

9. Fayette County Historical Society, "Tragic Springer House Fire," *The Fayette Gazette* (First Quarter, 2016): 1–4; Liz Zemba, "Loss of Historic Fayette Farmhouse Blamed on Vandals," *TribLive* (Tarentum, PA), April 28, 2015, https://archive.triblive.com/news/loss-of-historic-fayette-farmhouse-blamed-on-vandals/.

10. Pugh, "Reminiscences of an Old Fogey," MS 00011.

11. See "Almira Frost," MyHeritage, accessed April 22, 2019, https://www.myheritage.com/names/almira_frost; "Message Boards, Ragan Family," Ancestry, accessed December 5, 2019, https://www.ancestry.com.au/boards/localities.northam.usa.states.louisiana.parishes.lafourche/208; "James Frost-Phoebe Greene," Ball's Place blog; and Cynthia Daigle, "Authement, Fatchette, Savoie, Daigle Connection," RootsWeb's World Connect Community Trees Index, accessed April 22, 2019, http://wc.rootsweb.ancestry.com/cgi-bin/igm.cgi?db=cynthiadaigle [website no longer active, as of December 17, 2025].

[12]. Pierre Lefebvre acquired the twenty arpent-wide parcel, referred to as "une habitation sur la bayou Lafourche," in 1818 from the lawyer and diplomat Edward Livingston. Lafourche Parish Original Acts, COB B, 1818–1821, fol. 160.

[13]. For the Lefebvre accounting and the civil suits against him by Springer and Frost, see MS-00188, Accessions 066–0004–001 and 006–004–007, 1839–1841, Nicholls State University Archives; and Lafourche Parish, LA, Records, Civil Suit 737 (Springer vs. Lefebvre), and Civil Suit 738 (Frost vs. Lefebvre), both 2nd J. D. Court, in 1841.

[14]. MS-00188, Accession 024–005–037, Nicholls State University Archives.

[15]. For the Jackson Street lot transactions of Guion, et al, see Lafourche Parish, LA, Records, COB S, fols. 192 & 193 (February 1, 1843); COB U, fol. 473 (May 24, 1845); COB V, fol. 147 (November 25, 1845); and COB W, fol. 253 (March 13, 1846).

[16]. For a description of how Frost and Springer acquired their workshop property, see Lafourche Parish, LA, Records COB X, fols. 560, 563, and 566 (March 11, 15, and 16, 1845).

[17]. Lafourche Parish, LA, Records, COB W, fol. 343(October 23, 1845).

[18]. Lafourche Parish, LA, Records, COB S, fol. 386 (January 9, 1844); COB DD, fol. 306 (December 16, 1850); and COB 1, fol. 8 (January 11, 1854). Master builders considered their tools among their most precious belongings. Frost possessed "three chest[s] of Carpenter's tools," which his estate valued at $1,111; in contrast, a Frost family horse was worth only $175. Lafourche Parish, LA, Records, COB 1, fol. 8 (January 11, 1854).

[19]. Lafourche Parish, LA, Records, COB 1, fols. 5 and 8 (January 11, 1854); Lafourche Parish, LA, Records, Miscellaneous Book 1, January 10, 1854. There is no record of the fate of William, the third enslaved carpenter acquired by Van P. Winder from the Frost succession.

Chapter Six

[1]. Donald J. Hébert, *South Louisiana Church and Civil Records, Lafourche-Terrebonne Parishes,* vol. 2: 1841–1850 (Donald J. Hébert, 1978), 360; "My Father's Ancestors and Their Descendants, 10 July 2015," RootsWeb's World Connect Community Trees Index, accessed August 25, 2015, https://rootsweb.ancestry.com/cgi.bin/igm.cgi?op=GET+db=mfaatdob1515+id=I14358 [website no longer active, as of December 17, 2025].

[2]. *The Lafourche Comet* (Thibodaux, LA), July 18, 1918 (Microfilm, Nicholls State University Archives); Philip Chauvin Jr. and Phoebe Chauvin Morrison, *1880 U.S. Census, Lafourche Parish, LA* (Terrebonne Genealogical Society, Inc., 1999), 18. Azelie's surname, Bourg, rather than that of her father, Joseph Guillot,

is not explained. Among Morgan and Azelie Clementine's children, Marie Clara, or Clara, born 1854, lived longest, her death occurring in 1936. In 1877 she married the Rev. Charles D. F. Lyne, an English-born priest at St. John's Episcopal Church in Thibodaux. He died in 1886 at Key West, Florida, where he had served at St. Paul's Episcopal Church. *The Lafourche Comet*, July 18, 1918; Herman Cope Duncan, *The Diocese of Louisiana, Some of Its History, 1838–1888: Also Some of the History of Its Parishes and Missions, 1805–1888* (A. W. Hyatt, 1888), 252; Jefferson Beale Brown, *Key West: The Old and the New* (The Record Company, 1912), 29; Denis Gaubert, "A Story, Part II: The Rev. Charles Felix Dixon Lyne," *St. John's Historic Cemetery Association Newsletter* (Fall 2023), https://www.stjhca.org/visit-1.html.

3. Chauvin and Morrison *1880 U.S. Census,* 19.

4. George S. Guion to Morgan Springer, COB S, fol. 193 (February 1, 1843).

5. Advertisements, *The Thibodaux Minerva*, September 3, 1853, and September 2, 1854.

6. Thomas M. Williams to James Frost and Morgan Springer, COB X, fol. 500 (March 11, 1847).

7. John Larkin to James Frost and Morgan Springer, COB X, fol. 563 (March 5, 1847).

8. Charles Hawley to James Frost and Morgan Springer, COB X, fol. 573 (March 16, 1847).

9. James Frost and Morgan Springer to Sciotha S. Evans, COB Y, fol. 123 (April 19, 1847).

10. The builders about whom this book is written (except for John Bellsen, living in Assumption) often voted in the yearly Thibodaux elections. Their participation was inconsistent, perhaps because of illness or work away from the town on those days. See, e. g., Town of Thibodaux Council Records, Book 1, May 3, 1849, May 3, 1852, and May 3, 1853. Voter counts for town officials varied, as low as 41 on May 4, 1840, to as high as 165 on May 5, 1856. See Town of Thibodaux Council Records, Book 1.

11. Martin, *Records and Recollections*, 17–18; Town of Thibodaux Council Records, Book 1, March 20, 1847, and August 5, 1848.

12. MS-00188, Accession 177–012–001 (June 11, 1847), Nicholls State University Archives.

13. Sale from James Frost to Morgan Springer, December 16, 1850, Lafourche Parish, LA, Records, COB DD, fol. 306 (December 16, 1850).

14. Inventory, Succession of James Frost, Lafourche Parish, LA, Records, COB 1, fol. 8 (January 11, 1854).

15. 1850 United States Federal Census.

16. 1860 United States Federal Census.

17. 1860 United States Federal Census, Slave Schedules.

18. *The Weekly Thibodaux Sentinel* (death notices), November 19, 1870, and February 11, 1899.

19. Sale from James Frost and Morgan Springer to S. S. Evans, Lafourche Parish, LA, Records, COB Y, fol. 123 (April 19, 1847).

20. Sale from S. S. Evans to John McCulla, Lafourche Parish, LA, Records, COB 22, Fol. 576 (March 4, 1886).

21. Henry Fleming vs. S. S. Evans, Lafourche Parish, LA, Records, COB Z, fol. 408 (June 29, 18480. H(enry) Fleming, who sued Evans on the promissory notes, was identified in *The Thibodaux Minerva* of September 2, 1854, "Town Directory," as a "Plain and Ornamental Plasterer, on Church Street."

22. "Sciotha S. Evans," Louisiana, U.S. Compiled Marriage Index, 1718–1925, Ancestry, accessed June 6, 2023, https://www.ancestry.com/search/collections/7837/; 1850 US Federal Census.

23. 1860 US Federal Census.

24. Cenac and Joller, *Hard Scrabble to Hallelujah,* 57ff.

25. Slave Sale, Van P. Winder to Morgan Springer & Susto S. Evans, Lafourche Parish, LA, Records COB 1, fol. 5 (January 19, 1854).

26. Cenac and Joller, *Hard Scrabble to Hallelujah*, 64–65.

27. Inventory, September 9, 1861, Estate of Morgan Springer, #602 Probate Records, Lafourche Parish, LA, Records. In Springer's 1861 succession inventory the enslaved artisan Aaron's age, noted as thirty, and Dan's age, as twenty-eight, conflict with their Winder sale ages given in 1854. At the time that Winder bought them, in 1854, the men were described having ages thirty and twenty-five, but there can be little doubt that they were the same persons.

28. Telephone communication Richard Bourgeois to David D. Plater, September 28, 2025.

Chapter Seven

1. Henry French Brownlee, abstractor and transcriber, and Maggie Stewart, editor and formatter, "1850 Federal Census Lafourche Parish, Louisiana (File 4 of 11)," USGenWeb Census Project, 2006, http://files.usgwarchives.net/la/lafourche/census/1850/pg294a.txt.

2. Minutes, Thibodaux Town Council Records, Book 1, 1838–1862; Lafourche Parish, Louisiana, Laws & Ordinances, No. 1.

[3.] "Improvements," *The Thibodaux Minerva,* August 6, 1853, p. 2.

[4.] Receipt, January 13, 1857, MS-00188, Accession 085–006–001, Nicholls State University Archives.

[5.] Minutes, Thibodaux Town Council Records, Book 1, 1838–1862, February 21, 1855, May 8, 1858, and August 5, 1859.

[6.] Grisamore, "Fifty Years Ago."

[7.] Martin, *Records and Recollections,* 39; *The Intelligencer, and Lafourche and Terrebonne Advertiser,* February 3, 1837; and Charles M. Menard, *Annals of the Church of St. Joseph,* trans. in *The Bayou Catholic* (Historical Research Center of the Diocese of Houma-Thibodaux, Thibodaux, LA), 1842, both cited in Plater, ed., *"The Remarkably Neat Church,"* 25.

[8.] Lafourche Parish Police Jury Record D, 1852–1862, 10, 15, 18, 21 [hereafter cited as Lafourche PJ Record D].

[9.] Lafourche PJ Record D, 26, 43.

[10.] Born in Maine around 1805, Sumner Townsend shared with Arthur M. Foley ownership of the sawmill by the mid-1840s. The mill went through several ownerships after 1860, and Townsend purchased it again from John S. Adams in July 1869 for $2,500. In November 1869, Townsend sold to the "Foundry Building" owners, Beattie & Hare, a small portion of the sawmill lot in November 1869, for $800; and, finally, he sold the remaining sawmill property in February 1870, to Lawrence Keefe of Lafourche. This transaction included a release of the interest owned by Townsend's wife, Ruth Webster Eaton. (An earlier wife, named Elvira Gould, died in Thibodaux at an unknown date.) Townsend eventually returned to New England, where on December 25, 1881, he died in Boston. See "Sumner Townsend," WikiTree; Lafourche Parish, LA, Records, COB 12, fol. 389; COB 13, fol. 73; and COB 13, fol. 191.

[11.] Lafourche PJ Record D, 54, 61, 63, 68, 73.

[12.] For Howard's work on St. John's, see Building Contract, Parish of St. John's, Lafourche Parish, LA, Records, Miscellaneous Book 2, 175 (June 11, 1856); and Brantley and McGee, *Henry Howard,* 157, n. 58.

[13.] Lafourche Parish PJ Record D, 77.

[14.] Lafourche Parish PJ Record D, 91.

[15.] Lafourche Parish PJ Record D, 93–96.

[16.] On Bellsen's role at St. Matthew's Episcopal Church in Houma, see MS 000207, E.P., Box 24, St. Matthew's Episcopal Church Records, April 25, 1859, 20–21, Nicholls State University Archives, Thibodaux, LA. Reverend Thomas R. B. Trader, of Maryland and the minister at St. John's Thibodaux from 1854 to 1869, helped organize and raise money for St. Matthew's and influenced the choice of Howard's firm for its design. Plater, ed., "*The Remarkably Neat Church,*"

72–74; "Louisiana Intelligence," *Times-Picayune* (New Orleans), June 28, 1857, p. 2, https://www.newspapers.com/image/25780585/.

17. Agreement between John Bellsen and the Lafourche Parish Police Jury, May 5, 1858, Accession No. 032–005–003, Nicholls State University Archives.

18. Lafourche Parish PJ Record D, 111, 123–24.

19. Agreement, John Bellsen and the Lafourche Parish Police Jury, No. 032–005–003.

20. Agreement, John Bellsen and the Lafourche Parish Police Jury, No. 032–005–003; Lafourche PJ Record D, 91, 93, 94–95, 96, 111, 123–124, 135, 136, and 137.

21. Brantley and McGee, *Henry Howard*, 157.

22. Resolution No. 64, Lafourche Parish, LA, Laws and Ordinances No. 1, 76.

23. P. A. Champomier, *Statement of the Sugar Crop Made in Louisiana in 1845–1846* (New Orleans: n.p., 1846), 21. Digital copy from the Seligman Collection, Rare Book and Manuscript Library, Columbia University, accessed August 2, 2023, https://archive.org/details/ldpd_6413611_000. Champomier states that Bellsen partnered with a neighbor, named Ford, on another small tract nearby.

24. Bellsen family information, all accessed May 23, 2023, available through www.Findagrave.com, are "John Bellsen," Memorial ID 22923549; "Sarah Elizabeth Barbre Bellsen," Memorial ID 22923546; and "Vedder J. Bellsen," Memorial ID 40196169. See also "John Bellsen," 1860 United States Federal Census, Ancestry, https://www.ancestry.com/search/collections/7667/; "John Bellsen," Louisiana, U.S. Compiled Marriage Index, 1718–1925, Ancestry, https://www.ancestry.com/search/collections/7837/; 1870 United States Federal Census.

25. Assumption Parish, LA, Records, Miscellaneous No. 13, Fol. 201 (December 13, 1853).

26. Brantley and McGee, *Henry Howard*, 51–62, 281.

27. Resolution No. 22, June 6, 1859, Lafourche Parish Laws and Ordinances No. 1, 39–41.

28. Resolution No. 27, July 18, 1859, Lafourche Parish Laws and Ordinances, No. 1, 44.

29. Brantley and McGee, *Henry Howard*, 184, 186, and notes 116, 117, and 118.

30. Minutes, Thibodaux Town Council Records, May 4, 1857, May 10, 1858, and May 1859.

31. Resolution No. 36, December 5, 1859, Lafourche Parish Laws & Ordinances No. 1, 50–52. Rather than having become the jailor's house, the original courthouse was moved. In 1890, Silas Grisamore, observed that the old courthouse "is now occupied by James A. Frost as a saloon." Frost—a son of the original migrant—located it to the north diagonally opposite the new courthouse

on the Green and Market Streets corner. Martin, *Records and Recollections*, 39. The scrap from the old courthouse was sold for $400 to J. M. Lowenstein. June 30, 1861, Session, Lafourche PJ Record D, 155.

32. Lafourche PJ Record D, 137, 140, 148, 154, 159.

33. Probate Inventory, Lafourche Parish, LA, Succession Records No. 602, Estate of Morgan Springer.

34. Brantley and McGee, *Henry Howard*, 184, 186–187, 190, 195–201, 272; Louisiana vs. Thiberge, No. 159, 15th JDC, Lafourche Parish, LA, Accession 111–003–001 (1875), Nicholls State University Archives. The Thiberge trial file includes advertisements in *The Weekly Thibodaux Sentinel* publicizing Thiberge's presence as a working architect in the town in 1877 and 1878. Information on Thiberge's pardon by Kellogg and his hiring by Dr. Dansereau is not included in the file, but on October 14, 1876, *The Weekly Thibodaux Sentinel* announced that Thiberge's death sentence was to be commuted by Governor Kellogg after December 17, when his six-month jail term in the Lafourche Parish Jail ended. Besides having drawn plans for the Dansereau House during that incarceration, Thiberge created plans for St. Mary Catholic Church located above Raceland, facing Bayou Lafourche. See *The Weekly Thibodaux Sentinel*, October 14, 1876; March 24, 1877; November 9, 1878; and November 11, 1893.

35. For Thiberge's 1879 work on the Lafourche parish jail and courthouse, see Lafourche Parish Records, Miscellaneous Book 6, fol. 35; and Bond Book 1, fol. 161.Newspaper advertisements evidence Thiberge's return to New Orleans beginning 1880–1881, at first in practice alone at 16 Carondelet Street, then at 13 Commercial Place, and thereafter with Howard at 13 Commercial Place through December 1882. See *The New Orleans Democrat*, May 22, 1880, September 1, 1881, September 10, 1881, September 23, 1882, and December 22, 1882. A copy of Thiberge's plans for the Dansereau House is in the Nicholls State University Archives, MS 00029, "Lafourche American Revolution Bicentennial Commission and Lafourche Heritage Collection." It was donated to the university archives by Mrs. V. L. Caldwell, a one-time owner of the Dansereau House.

36. Clifton Theriot to David D. Plater, e-mail October 8, 2020.

37. "Specifications of a Building for a Parish Court House to be erected in the town of Thibodaux, La," MS-00188, Accession No. 177–013–001, Nicholls State University Archives; Martin, *Records and Recollections*, 18, 26–29, 36. See Appendix A herein.

38. Phoebe Chauvin Morrison, comp., *1860 Census, Lafourche Parish, LA* (Terrebonne Genealogical Society, 2001).

39. "Specifications of a Building," MS-00188, Accession No. 177–013–001.

40. "Specifications of a Building," MS-00188, Accession No. 177–013–001.

41. Brantley and McGee, *Henry Howard*, 184, 186–187, 296, Ch. 4 n. 118.

Chapter Eight

1. Marriage Book 1839, Lafourche Parish, LA, Records; Roderick H. Burnham, *The Burnham Family; or, Genealogical Records of the Descendants of the Four Emigrants of the Name, Who Were Among the Early Settlers in America* (Hartford, CT: Press of Case, Lockwood, & Leonard, 1869), 89, accessed July 21, 2023, www.familysearch.org/library/books/idviewer/374161. The Burnham parents' birth and death dates tend to vary in the cited sources.

2. For more on both Collins and Hawley, see Plater, ed., *"The Remarkably Neat Church,"* 48–49, 57–58.

3. "Shubael Tenney: A Story," *St. John's Historic Cemetery Association Newsletter* (February–March 2018), https://www.stjhca.org/visit-1.html.

4. Lafourche Parish, LA, Records, COB M, Fol. 499 (February 6, 1837).

5. Lafourche Parish Civil Suits, Joseph R. Niles vs. Edward T. Burnham, No. 646 (1837); *The Thibodaux Minerva*, September 3, 1853; *Terrebonne Life Lines* 19, no. 2 (Summer 2000), 116 [quoting *The Thibodaux Minerva*, May 6, 1854]. Scudday's acquisition was of lots 9 and 41, totaling 73,057 square feet, or about 1.68 acres. Lafourche Parish, LA, Records, COB S, fol. 91 (May 12, 1842). Name spellings varied, e.g., Jake Weber was also Jacob Webre.

6. Lafourche Parish, LA, Records, COB N, Fol. 103 (Partnership Burnham/Randel, March 18, 1837).

7. Lafourche Parish, LA, Civil Suit Records, No. 792 (Niles vs. Burnham), and Civil Suit No. 896 (Burnham vs. Randal, 1840–1843).

8. Lafourche Parish, LA, Records, COB U, fol. 74 (Annulment of Partnership, April 16, 1844).

9. Lafourche Parish, LA, Records, COB O, fol. 470 (January 17, 1839).

10. Lafourche Parish, LA, Records, COB S, fol. 366 (October 23, 1843).

11. Lafourche Parish, LA, Records, COB S, Fol. 111 (July 20, 1842).

12. Lafourche Parish, LA, Civil Suit Records, Civil Suit 949, Second Judicial District Court (1844).

13. Lafourche Parish Civil Suit Records, Civil Suit 949. Along with Burnham, a recent arrival, Benjamin Franklin (B. F.) Holden, a native of Maine, ran a Thibodaux grocery store on Market (now West Second) Street. In the 1850s he owned the Franklin House hotel, "on the corner of St. Louis Street and Commercial Row." Holden also captained a steamboat and operated a livery service to transport railroad passengers to and from Lafourche Crossing. "The Benjamin Franklin Holdens: A Story," *St. John's Historic Association Newsletter* (February–March 2020), https://www.stjhca.org/visit-1.html; Franklin House Ad, *Thibodaux Minerva*, September 3, 1853, p. 1.

14. Lafourche Parish, LA, Civil Suit Records, Civil Suit No. 71, Fifth Judicial Court (March 3, 1845).

15. For various transactions involving people whom Burnham held in bondage, including Betsy and Kitty, see Lafourche Parish Records, LA, COB U, fol. 438

(May 13, 1845), COB 2, fol. 20 (December 29, 1847), COB GG, Fol. 2 (January 25, 1853), COB FF, Fol. 412 (March 3, 1853), and COB 3, Fol. 383 (May 7, 1856); and in Terrebonne Parish, LA, Conveyance Records, COB OA 4, fol. 439 (August 14, 1855). See also Westerman, *Lafourche Parish, Louisiana, Census 1850*, Dwelling No. 384.

16. See Burnham's acquisitions of enslaved workers, all in Lafourche Parish, LA, Records: COB FF, fol. 324 (January 14, 1853), COB 2, fol. 636 (January 14, 1856), COB BB, fol. 74 (February 17, 1849), COB BB, fol. 558 (March 4, 1850), COB CC, fol. 784 (January 14, 1853), and COB GG, fol. 34 (March 28, 1853).

17. Minutes, Thibodaux Town Council Records, Book 1, March 2 and May 1, 1847.

18. Minutes, Thibodaux Town Council Records, Book 1, December 8, July 13, July 22, and July 24, 1848; and March 10, May 7, September 16, and October 26, 1849.

19. Building Contract, July 24, 1848, MS-00188, Accession 177–012–004; Martin, *Records and Recollections*, 43, 44, 47.

20. Lafourche Parish, LA, Records, COB BB, fol. 412 (January 4, 1850), COB BB, fol. 531 (February 23, 1850).

21. Lafourche Parish, LA, Records, COB 1, fol. 304 (April 29, 1854).

22. Terrebonne Parish, LA, Conveyance Records, COB Q.17, fol. 204 (July 19, 1854).

23. Phoebe Chauvin Morrison, annotator. *Re-Annotated 1860 Census of Terrebonne Parish, Louisiana. June 4, 1860.* (Terrebonne Genealogical Society, 1992), 67.

24. Terrebonne Parish, LA, Conveyance Records, Inventory, Succession of Lucy D. Breaux, COB U, Fol. 612 (March 10, 1863, rec. March 23, 1863).

25. Terrebonne Parish, LA, Records, Family Meeting, Succession of Lucy D. Breaux, COB U, Fol. 616 (March 11, 1863, rec. March 27, 1863).

26. Morrison, *1860 Census*; Phoebe Chauvin Morrison, annotator, *1870 Census Terrebonne Parish, LA* (Terrebonne Genealogical Society, 2002).

27. Plater, ed., *"The Remarkably Neat Church,"* 6–7, 14–17.

28. Brantley and McGee, *Henry Howard*, 138. The contract between St. John's and Burnham is recorded in Miscellaneous Book 2, 175–183, and in Original Acts (1856), fol. 1468, both in the Lafourche Parish, LA, Records. Neither source includes drawings, which remain undiscovered. Further reference to the renovation work may be considered as documented here.

29. Stuart Morgan, "A Belief in the Power of Concealed Shoes: Investigating the Age-Old Superstition of Hiding Footwear Within the Structure of a Building," *Satra Bulletin* (May 2018): 50, https://www.Satra.com/bulletin/article.php?id=2078.

30. Building Contract, Lafourche Parish, LA, Records, Miscellaneous Book 2, 175–183.

31. For their comments about the church renovation, see Brantley and McGee, *Henry Howard*, 138–140. And on the church bell installed in 1856, see Plater, ed., "*The Remarkably Neat Church*," 17. For an advertisement showing what—besides "seasoned lumber"—the local sawmill offered as of 1856, see *The Thibodaux*

Minerva, November 5, 1853. On the enslaved man Bob's purchase in 1854, see Terrebonne Partish, LA, Conveyance Records, COB Q-17, fol. 140, and Official Acts 3. fol. 227 (April 22, 1854).

32. Building Contract, Miscellaneous Book 2, Lafourche Parish, LA, Records, 175–183.

33. Martin, *Records and Recollections*, 25–29; Lafourche Parish, LA, Records, Original Acts 1468 (August 1, 1856).

34. Martin, *Records and Recollections*, 25–29; Lafourche Parish, LA, Records, Original Acts 1468 (August 1, 1856).

35. Charles Gardener, comp., *Gardener's New Orleans Dictionary for 1861* (New Orleans: Charles Gardener, 1861), 50. Avaiable through the Civil War Philatelic Society, accessed October 27, 2017, https://www.civilwarphilatelicsociety.org/wp-content/uploads/2019/06/Res-Arch-Dir-New-Orleans-Dir-1861.pdf. The name of the engineer, Nelson, was unlisted; *The New Orleans Crescent,* September 3, 1856, citing *The Thibodaux Minerva.*

36. Lafourche Parish, LA, Records, Miscellaneous Book 2, February 6 and 11, 1857, fols. 256 ff.

37. Information on the St. Tammany Parish's Poitevent family is from a Poitevent family descendant, Ann Parkerson Burke, of Mandeville, LA., by telephone to the author.

38. Lafourche Parish, LA, Records, Miscellaneous Book 2 (February 6 and 11, 1857); Terrebonne Parish, LA, Records, Slave Sales, COB R, 456 and 473 (February 4 and 18, 1857).

Epilogue

1. Lafourche Parish Laws & Ordinances No. 1, Resolution #13, September 6, 1838, 32.

2. *New Orleans Crescent*, May 5, 1857, from *The Thibodaux Minerva*, May 2, 1857. For discussion of the activities of members of the American Party in another Louisiana town, Clinton, see Thompson, *Clinton, Louisiana*, 45–47.

3. Lafourche Parish, LA, Records, Succession of Absalom Kees, Probate No. 883. The Kees Succession was difficult, lengthy, and at times contentious among his family. It required extensive testimony for proof of death, and the parish court judgment closing the succession did not occur until 1877.

4. For the 1860 Census figures and Louise Delphine Burnham's death date, see Terrebonne Parish Genealogical Society Census Committee, *The Terrebonne Parish 1860 Census, June 4 1860* (Terrebonne Parish Genealogical Society, 1983), 121. For family information, see Burnham, *The Burnham Family,* 103.

5. Burnham, *The Burnham Family*, 104–105.

6. Not all of Burnham's daughters escaped to Connecticut in 1863, as claimed by Burnham. Among the official military records of E. T. Burnham made available by Ms. Browning (e-mail from Laura Browning, Houma, LA, June 7–8, 2019) is a letter from Burnham dated January 15, 1865, to the post adjutant, Captain Jackson, requesting a leave of absence for forty-eight hours "to go to Terrebonne Station to see a daughter who is at the point of death." She may have been Julia, listed as age fifteen in the 1860 Census. Burnham's son Edward supposedly joined the Union forces in 1862. Some of the children did settle in Connecticut: Sarah Felicia Burnham (1842–1938), Katherine Collins Burnham (1853–1942), Ellen Maria Burnham (1856–1924), and Louisa Delphine Burnham (1859–?). All are buried in Cedar Hill Cemetery, Hartford. See "Sarah F. Burnham," Docufree CemeteryFind, accessed May 15, 2023, https://www.cemeteryfind.com/PublicSearch/BurialSearch; "Miss Sarah F. Burnham Funeral," *Hartford Courant,* May 16, 1938, p. 4; "Katherine Collins 'Kate' Burnham Stebbins," Find a Grave, accessed September 26, 2022, https://www.findagrave.com/memorial/27480153/katherine-collins-stebbins; "Ellen Maria Burnham Biddle," Find a Grave, accessed May 16, 2023, https://findagrave.com/memorial/27479931/ellen-maria-biddle; "Louisa Delphine Burnham Birmingham, Find a Grave, accessed September 26, 2022, https://www.findagrave.com/memorial/27479938/louisa-delphine-birmingham.

7. Burnham, *The Burnham Family*, 105.

8. Miscellaneous official records of Captain E. T. Burnham's service with the Ninety-Eighth US Colored Infantry, by e-mail from Laura Browning. See also US War Department, *The War of the Rebellion: A Compilation of the Official Records of the Union and Confederate Armies,* Series I, Vol. XLI, Part IV (Government Printing Office, 1880–1901; Republication, National Historical Society, 1971; Reprint, Historical Times, 1985), 975. For names and descriptions of a number of Union Army installations in the Lafourche District, see Powell A. Casey, *Encyclopedia of Forts, Posts, Named Camps, and Other Military Installations in Louisiana, 1700–1981.* (Claitor's Publishing Division, 1983), 4 (Algiers), 32 (Boutte Station), 32–33 (Brashear City), 102 (Lafourche Crossing), 40 (Chacahoula), 76 (Thibodaux), 230 (Terrebonne Station), and 127 (Napoleonville).

9. For Burnham's Iberia Parish Republican connections, the convention of 1872, and his death information, see *New Orleans Republican*, May 21, 1872, p. 5, and June 2, 1872, p. 3, obtained by email courtesy DeeDee DiBenedetto, June 13, 2019.

10. *Terrebonne Life Lines* 18, no. 4 (Winter 1999), 259, citing *The Weekly Thibodaux Sentinel*, August 31, 1878; and "Capt. Edward Truman Burnham," Find A Grave, accessed August 6, 2023, www.findagrave.com/memorial/76015621/edward-truman-burnham.

11. 1870 United States Federal Census, courtesy DeeDee Dibenedetto by e-mail May 23, 2023.

12. "Sarah Elizabeth Barbre Bellsen," Find a Grave, accessed May 23, 2023, www.findagrave.com/memorial/22923566.

13. "News Items," *St. Charles Herald* (Hahnville, LA), October 24, 1885, p. 2, courtesy DeeDee Dibenedetto, by email June 5, 2023

14. "Lelia 'Lee' Bellsen McCoy," Find a Grave, accessed August 2, 2023, www.findagrave.com/memorial/661711773/lelia-mccoy.

15. *Fort Worth Gazette*, June 7, 1891, p. 12, courtesy DeeDee Dibenedetto by email June 5, 2023; *San Antonia Daily Light*, October 27, 1896, courtesy DeeDee Dibenedetto by email June 5, 2023; John Bellsen's gravestone in the Beeville Cemetery shows his death year as 1897, "John Bellsen," Find a Grave, accessed August 2, 2023, www.findagrave.com/memorial/22923549/john-bellsen.

16. Lafourche Parish, LA, Records, COB Y, fol. 123 (04/19/1847).

17. Lafourche Parish, LA, Records, Civil Suit 539, Succession of George S. Guion vs. Sciotha S. Evans; Lafourche Parish, LA, records, COB 12, fol. 337 (May 4, 1869); *Plan of Thibodaux Saw Mill, March 4, 1869*, tracing dated April 22, 1927, J. A. and J. C. Lovell Collection, MS-00085. Nicholls State University Archives and Special Collections, Thibodaux, LA.

18. *The Weekly Thibodaux Sentinel*, November 19, 1870, p. 2.

19. St. John's Episcopal Church Cemetery Listings, Library of St. John's Episcopal Church, Thibodaux, LA; "Mary J. Evans," Find a Grave, accessed August 11, 2023, https://www.findagrave.com/memorial/23452177/mary-j-evans. Of note regarding the early Evans family connection with St. John's Episcopal Church, an Evans child, Catherine Collins, was baptized there on May 1, 1854; another daughter, Julia Francis, was married in the church to Wayne Tanner on December 5, 1860. Hébert, *South Louisiana Records,* vol. 3, 116.

20. 1880 United States Federal Census.

21. For the sale of the Evans family property in Thibodaux, see Lafourche Parish, La, Records, COB 22, fol. 576 (March 4, 1886).

22. "Sciotha S Evans," Find a Grave, accessed August 2, 2023, www.findagrave.com/memorial/60330347/sciotha-s-evans.

23. Smith, *White Pillars*, 233.

24. Smith, *White Pillars*, 220.

25. Brantley and Magee, *Henry Howard,* 15.

26. Smith, *White Pillars*, 228.

27. Eric Sloane, *A Museum of Early American Tools* (Ballentine Books, 1974), xii.

28. Walt Whitman, "I Hear America Singing," *Leaves of Grass* (New York: W.E. Chapin & Co., Printers, 1867), 308.

Index

The letter *f* following a page locator denotes a figure, *p* a photograph, and *m* a map.

C

T

www.ingramcontent.com/pod-product-compliance
Lightning Source LLC
LaVergne TN
LVHW010029250626
841832LV00006B/24

* 9 7 8 1 9 5 9 5 6 9 3 6 7 *